Pacific Search Press

The Salmon Cookbook

by Jerry Dennon

Pacific Search Press, 715 Harrison Street, Seattle, Washington 98109
© 1978 by Jerden Industries, Inc. All rights reserved
Printed in the United States of America

Edited by Deborah Easter
Designed by Paula Schlosser
Illustrated by Darci Covington

Library of Congress Cataloging in Publication Data

Dennon, Jerry.
    The salmon cookbook.
    Includes index.
    1. Cookery (Salmon) I. Title.
TX747.D46   641.6'9'2   77-25088
ISBN 0-914718-30-4

Contents

Acknowledgments

I would like to thank the following for their assistance in preparing this book: C. Reid Rogers, James Nevarre, Pete Harris, Conrad Mahnken, A. J. Novotny, Ralph Munro, Ed Young, Jon Lindbergh, Tom Stockley, Harlan Freeman, Cindy Bonnington, Don Mowat, Brian Allee, the California Wine Board, the National Marine Fisheries Service, and the Washington Department of Fisheries.

Introduction

An Indian gave me a piece of fresh salmon roasted, which I ate with relish. This was the first salmon I had seen and it convinced me we were in the waters of the Pacific Ocean.

From the journal of Meriwether Lewis at the headwaters of the Lehmi River, 3 August 1805

An archaeological expedition to southern France discovered the first known record of salmon. A picture had been carved on a reindeer bone by an ancestor of ours some ten to fifteen thousand years ago. This graphic record indicates that salmon was known and valued by man when the reindeer roamed over France and the great glacial ice sheet covered most of Europe.

It was long after the glaciers had receded that the Imperial Roman legions, on their march to the conquest of Britain about 56 B.C., camped on the banks of the Garonne River in Gaul. Here they first saw the mighty salmon leap. They christened this new fish the "Leaper" or "Salmo" (the English word "salmon" is derived from the Latin *salire*, to leap), and it soon found its way to the Roman stomach. Indeed, in A.D. 77, Pliny wrote that "the river salmon is preferred to all fish that swim in the sea."

The salmon has maintained this lofty status down through the centuries. Salt salmon was an important item of trade between Scotland and England in the seventeenth century. And, during the eighteenth century (after the advent of packing in ice) salmon shipped from Scotland to London was valued more highly than beefsteak.

In America, salmon was a revered staple food of the west coast Indians. When feeling the pinch of hunger after the long winter, the Indians greeted the first salmon runs with great rejoicing. The Indians believed their gods sent the fish to them each year so they expressed their gratitude with special religious ceremonies. They also found salmon of economic value; after frying it, they pounded it to a fine powder that was a prized article of trade with the plains Indians. At that time, salmon was to the coastal tribes what buffalo was to those of the plains.

Today, salmon is still a nutritious staple in the diet of many peoples, with the world harvest of all species running a little under one billion pounds live weight—at first glance a tremendous amount. Private experiments in salmon aquaculture, or farming, under the supervision of the United States Marine Fisheries Service, have also produced a delightful variation of the commercially harvested full-grown salmon—the pan-sized fish—which has become a gourmet specialty in some areas. This innovative process involves raising the salmon in saltwater cages and not allowing them to migrate to sea. These controlled conditions combined with a special diet produce a delicate and flavorful fish that is ready for market at eighteen months of age.

As much as man's demand for salmon has remained constant over the years, his concern for the species' survival has never equalled this demand. Salmon once thronged the rivers in North America, Europe, and Asia in such numbers that spawning runs caused the waters to overflow the banks and sometimes even upset small boats. Salmon was then an abundant and cheap source of food. But since the latter part of the nineteenth century, these runs have been shrinking yearly—as has the size of the commercial harvest. Although recent international agreements now give the Pacific and Atlantic species a measure of protection, the chairman of the New England Fish Company, C. Reid Rogers, stresses that there must be an ongoing effort to "minimize stream pollution, regulate catches, safeguard forests that provide clear water for streams, and assist nature through salmon hatchery programs." In other words, as throughout history, salmon must be accorded man's respect.

Spawning and Migration

Asian and North American salmon range and feed together in great thousand-mile gyres, in schools numbering in the millions throughout the North Pacific. Eventually they divide into families and split off from this great celebration of species to breed and spawn in specific homes in the great rivers and innumerable streams of the North Pacific Rim. The great rivers—the Columbia, the Fraser, the Skeena, the Stikine, the Yukon, the Anadyr, the Amur—are spawning homes for the ubiquitous salmon as well as drainage routes for vast portions of the planetary watershed.

Each school of salmon navigates unerringly back to the stream of its birth on a time schedule that can be predicted to within a few days. In general, North American salmon make this circular journey in a counterclockwise direction while Asian salmon move clockwise. Pinks make the circuit once and race home to spawn; sockeyes make it once each year for three or four years. The enormous schools travel at a general rate of ten miles per day until the spawning urge takes them and they increase their speed to thirty miles per day. The fish are nearly always found in the top thirty feet of water during the migrations.

No one really understands the mechanisms that guide the fish through the trackless ocean and back to a specific spot at a specific time. Evidence seems to indicate that the circuits are printed on the genes of the individual fish. It is unlikely that either a consciousness common to a school or memorized information guides them. The indisputable fact is: Salmon always find their way back to the streams or lakes where they were born and spawn there again, generation after generation.

As spawning salmon approach freshwater, they have reached the peak of their physical and instinctual genius. Fat and shining and leaping, schools swarm restlessly at the mouths of rivers and streams, waiting for optimal conditions of runoff. They feed voraciously, generally on herring, for they do not feed again once they enter freshwater. Before they head upstream is the time to take salmon for meat. The flavor and texture of the flesh is at its very best and when eaten fresh, the strength of the fish stays with the eater.

It is probable that the salmon use their keen sense of smell to identify their home estuary and to choose the right forks as they push upstream. In experiments, biologists have plugged the salmon's nostrils during this stage of their journey. Without a sense of smell, the spawning run tends to move in a random manner and the fish get lost.

The trip upstream is an enormous effort. Even in the absence of human improvements on the rivers, cataracts, rapids, and waterfalls must be overcome. Yet in spite of such obstacles, the fish travel between thirty and ninety miles a day until they reach the spawning ground. The salmon then undergo striking physiological changes. Humpbacks grow the hump for which they are named; dogs develop long, sharp teeth and their upper mandible grows out and extends down over the lower; sockeyes' bodies turn blood red and their heads turn an olive green. Basically, the fish turn dark and look bruised; the organisms begin to consume themselves. As the fish are drawing their last strength from ocean-gained fat, their flesh turns soft.

The salmon are now ready to perform the breathtaking dance for which their entire lives have been in preparation. As they reach their spawning home, the fish pair off, male and female. A courtship ensues, the male swimming back and forth over the female, as she prepares the nest or "redd." Rubbing and nudging her, the male periodically darts off to drive away other males. The female builds the nest with her tail, scooping out silt and smaller stones to a depth of twelve to eighteen inches and in an area twice the length of the fish. Finally, all that is left in the nest are larger stones. (The crevasses and fissures between the stones will provide shelter for the eggs, and will also allow enough cold water to flow through the eggs to maintain an even temperature.) When the nest is completed, the female assumes a rigid position over the center of it and the male approaches, curving his body against hers. Generally the actual mating is a "monogamous" procedure with one male serving one female. However, there is an extreme amount of male competition and it is not unheard of for a second male to contribute to the fertilization process. The eggs (which are a brilliant, translucent orange red) and the clouds of milt are deposited simultaneously. The sperm, which stays alive in the water for only seconds, must enter the egg through a single tiny pore or micropyle, which itself closes over in a matter of minutes. The nest is covered and the process is repeated, for a day or a week, until all the eggs are deposited. A single female deposits from two thousand to five thousand eggs, but only a small percentage of these hatch. The rest are eaten by fish or birds, attacked by fungi, or washed downstream.

After an incubation period of fifty days to three months, the "alevins" hatch out with yolk sacs still attached. The babies nestle in the gravel for several weeks until the yolk sac is gone and they have gained an inch in size. At this point, they emerge from the gravel as "fry," quick and light-shy. It is at this stage of development that life is most perilous; the small fish are vulnerable to hungry larger salmon, other fish, and water birds.

The fry feed at dawn and dusk and into the night on planktonic crustacea and nymphs and grow fastest in the summer when insects are plentiful. Most salmon remain in lakes and streams for one to two years, though pinks and dogs begin their journey to the sea in the first year, as fry.

Out of two million eggs, perhaps twenty thousand survive to make the migration to salt water, an epic event that involves millions of smolt (as the little salmon are called at this stage). On the Yukon River, running through Alaska and Canada, this journey can be as long as eighteen hundred miles, on the Amur River in Asia, seven hundred to eight hundred miles. The fish travel in schools to avoid predators. When approaching an obstacle (such as rapids or cataracts), the school reacts in unison as though trained to make such a mass response. The smolt spend three to five months in estuaries and bays, gradually acclimatizing to salt water before moving out to the open sea. These survivors then begin, once again, the circuitous pattern from river to ocean to river that has been the life cycle of salmon for eons.

Species

The Pacific salmon *(Oncorhynchus)* is to be distinguished from the Atlantic salmon *(Salmo)*. More than ninety-five percent of the world's salmon harvest comes from the North Pacific, less than five percent from the Atlantic. There is only one species of salmon that ranges and feeds in the Atlantic; there are six species in the North Pacific. The seven species of salmon are:

Oncorhynchus tshawytscha Range: Northern Hokkaido River, Japan, to the Sacramento River, United States. In general, this species goes by the name of Chinook on Washington State's Columbia River, king in Alaska, and spring or tyee on Puget Sound in Washington State. It is the largest of the salmon, averaging 22 pounds, but is on record as weighing as much as 100 pounds. Its life-span is four to six years. Chinook meat has a softer texture than that of the other species and is very rich in oil. Ranging from deep salmon to white in color, the Chinook's meat is usually higher priced than that of other varieties of salmon.

Oncorhynchus nerka Range: Fraser River, Canada, to the Kuril Islands, Soviet Union. Called by fishermen red or sockeye in Alaska, sockeye or blueback on Puget Sound, and blueback on the Columbia River, this variety is known as the salmon that loves a lake. Always seeking a river that has a snow-fed lake in its watershed, the young sockeye spends from one to two years of life in this freshwater lake. It has a life-span of four to six years and the adult weighs about seven pounds. The meat, which is deep salmon in color, breaks into medium flakes, is firm in texture, and has considerable oil.

Oncorhynchus kisutch Range: Monterey Bay, United States, to the Kamchatka Peninsula, Soviet Union. This species is commonly known as the medium red, coho, or silver. Smaller than the king but larger than the sockeye, this salmon weighs about eight pounds, but has been known to weigh as much as thirty pounds. Its meat is deep salmon in color but lighter than that of the sockeye. This species usually matures in three years.

Oncorhynchus gorbucha Range: Klamath River, United States, to Korea. Pink or humpy salmon is frequently used for canning. Smallest of all the salmon, it averages about four and one-half pounds in weight and has an invariable life-span of two years. Pink salmon meat is small-flaked and ranges from light to deep pink in color.

Oncorhynchus keta Range: Puget Sound, United States, to Korea. Least expensive of all the salmon when canned, chum or keta meat is lighter in color and has less oil than the other varieties; it is large-flaked and more coarsely textured. The chum's life period is from three to five years and its average weight is nine pounds.

Oncorhynchus masu Range: Inland and coastal waters near Japan. Not generally available in North America, the cherry or masu salmon is smaller in size than the coho. It weighs from four to eight pounds and spends one to two years in freshwater before roaming into the Pacific. The color of the species is lighter than North American salmon, and the fish is often compared to trout.

Salmo salar Range: Maine, United States, and Labrador, Canada, to the European coast. The Atlantic salmon has been known to weigh as much as fifty pounds; however, the average weight of game fish runs from ten to fifteen pounds. The Atlantic salmon is a silver, tapered fish with the sharp features resembling most salmon species. The entire length of its back is spotted with slightly greenish blue coloring and the belly is silver white. This salmon represents a very small percentage of the United State's commercial harvest.

Pan-Sized Salmon

by Jon Lindbergh

A salmon in its natural state is a wild animal. It roams free in the ocean and to catch it by classical means you must become an aquatic hunter. The abundance or scarcity of this prized fish has until recently depended on the seasons and the weather, natural cycles, and the depredations of man. But thousands of years ago, man on land advanced from a chancy hunting economy to a more managed agricultural economy. Why should we still rely today on hunting to provide our seafood? The answer is coming in the form of the science of mariculture: the farming of the sea.

In 1970 Domsea Farms, Inc. and the United States National Marine Fisheries Service, with the assistance of the Sea Grant Office, established a pilot study called the Pacific Salmon Aquaculture Program. We reared several hundred thousand salmon up to migratory size and instead of releasing the fish to forage at sea, placed them into floating net enclosures in Puget Sound in Washington State. The young salmon lazily wheeled around in the nets in great silvery schools, gorging themselves on specially prepared food.

That year, there were plenty of problems to disrupt the tranquillity of these early schools of farm-raised salmon. Dogfish sharks chewed holes in the nets from below and seabirds plunged in from above. Violent tidal currents racked and twisted the netting until parts of it gave way to release thousands of salmon into the open Sound. Surprisingly, many of the escaped fish remained around the fish farm, rising up to strike at handouts and scavenging food lost through the net floors. In spite of the problems, our salmon thrived and after eight to twelve months, they were ready for harvest. We decided on a weight of about three quarters of a pound for harvesting, one succulent yearling salmon to a dinner plate.

Salmon farmers are continuing to develop new techniques to bring farm-raised salmon to the market place. The best fish are selected and reared to maturity to be the parents of a superior strain of domesticated salmon, much as livestock have been selected in agriculture. Farm fish are given special supplements to their diet. One example is red crab, a shrimp-like creature caught off Latin America, which enhances the salmon's health, flesh coloration, and taste.

Prompt and skilled treatment of fish after they have been harvested is critical to good quality. A freshly killed salmon has no "fishy" odor or taste. On a salmon farm the fish are chill-killed in cold brine, which reduces their body temperature to just above freezing. The still cold salmon are quickly dressed and prepared for marketing so as to achieve the best possible quality for your culinary enjoyment.

Jon Lindbergh is vice president of Domsea Farms, Inc. and a pioneer in salmon farming.

Preparing Salmon

Cleaning and Dressing

Most of the fish sold in the market today are already cleaned and dressed. However, if you are a fisherman or are lucky enough to have a friend give you one of his catches, you will need some basic cleaning and dressing instructions. Follow these steps:

1. Wash the fish. Place the fish on a cutting board and with one hand hold the fish firmly by the head. Holding a knife almost vertical, scrape off the scales, starting at the tail and scraping toward the head. Be sure to remove all the scales around the fins and head.

2. With a sharp knife, cut the entire length of the belly from the vent to the head. Remove the intestines. Cut around the pelvic fins and remove them.

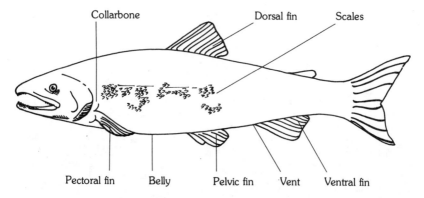

Collarbone   Dorsal fin   Scales

Pectoral fin   Belly   Pelvic fin   Vent   Ventral fin

3. Remove the head and the pectoral fins by cutting just back of the collarbone. If the backbone is large, cut down to it on each side of the fish. Then place the fish on the edge of the cutting board so that the head hangs over it, and snap the backbone by bending the head down. Cut any remaining flesh that holds the head to the body. Cut off the tail.

4. Remove the dorsal fin (the large fin on the back of the fish) by cutting along each side of the fin. Give a quick pull forward toward the head and remove the fin with the root bones attached. Remove the ventral fin in the same way. Never trim the fins off with shears or a knife because the root bones at the base of the fins will be left in the fish. Wash the fish thoroughly in cold running water. The fish is now dressed or pan-dressed, depending on its size.

5. To make steaks out of a large dressed fish, cut it crosswise into pieces about one inch thick.

6. In order to fillet a fish, you must have a sharp knife. First cut along the back of the fish from the tail to the head. Then cut down to the backbone just back of the collarbone. Turn the knife flat and cut the flesh away from the backbone and rib bones. Lift off the whole side of the fish or fillet in one piece. Turn the fish over and cut the fillet from the other side.

7. If you wish, you may skin the fillets. Place the fillet, skin side down, on a cutting board. Hold the tail end tightly with your fingers and, with a sharp knife, cut down through the flesh to the skin about one-half inch from the end of the fillet. Flatten the knife against the skin and cut the flesh away from the skin by sliding the knife forward while holding the tail end of the skin firmly between your fingers.

Freezing Your Catch

Begin by dressing the salmon (be sure to remove the head) and cutting it into desired roasts. Or, you can leave the fish whole if it is not over five to eight pounds. Wrap it in wax paper and then wrap it again in regular freezer paper or in heavy-duty foil. Be sure to cover the fish with several thicknesses and seal securely. Place the package into your freezer, which should be set at minus ten degrees.

Another method for freezing a fresh catch is to place the steaks singly in a flat pan, covering them completely with fresh, clean water. Place the pan in the freezer, which should be set at minus ten degrees. A half teaspoon of salt may be added to the water, but this must be remembered when salting the fish while cooking, or it may get too salty. After the fish is frozen, remove the ice block from the pan and wrap it in freezer paper. Your fish will keep indefinitely if you use this method.

Thawing

The most important aspect of thawing fish is to cook it soon after it is thawed. You should not hold thawed fish longer than a day before cooking.

Individual packages of fish should be placed *in the refrigerator* to thaw; allow twenty-four hours for a one-pound package. If a quicker thawing is necessary, place the individual packages under cold running water. It takes about one to two hours to thaw a one-pound package. You should never thaw fish at room temperature or in warm water, nor should you ever refreeze fish.

Fish portions or sticks should not be thawed before cooking. Some fish cuts, such as frozen fillets and steaks, do not require thawing as long as you allow additional cooking time. The same is true for pan-sized salmon. However, stuffed or breaded fillets should be thawed before cooking to ensure the best result.

Cooking Fish

Broiling: Fish steaks are usually turned once while broiling. The length of time depends on the size of the steak, fish, or fillet. A moderately hot broiler is best, 375 to 400 degrees. Brush with butter (margarine may be used if necessary), or place pieces of bacon over the fish, and set the fish two to six inches from the source of heat. Broil until the fish is well browned. Add salt and pepper after the fish is turned, or when the cooking is half-done. Fillets or steaks require about five to eight minutes on each side. Whole fish over an inch thick require about ten minutes. Split fish need not be turned; broil about six to eight minutes. Season whole fish with salt on the inside and brush lightly with salt and pepper on the outside, as well as with fat, before broiling.

Barbecuing: Charcoal broiling is a dry heat method of cooking over hot coals that has in recent years become a popular form of recreation. Fish, because they cook so quickly, are a natural for this method of cookery. Pan-dressed fish, fillets, and steaks are all suitable for charcoal broiling. If frozen, thaw the fish in advance. Because fish flake easily as their cooking nears completion, use of a well-greased, long-handled, hinged wire grill is recommended. Since charcoal broiling is a dry heat cooking method, thicker cuts of fish are preferable as they dry out less during the process than thin cuts. Also, to ensure serving juicy and flavorful fish, use a sauce that contains some fat and baste the fish generously before and while cooking. Fish are usually cooked about four inches from moderately hot coals for ten to twenty minutes, depending on the thickness of the fish.

Poaching: Wrap the fish in clean cheesecloth or muslin (a dish towel will do) and place it in a wire basket. Do not lay fillets or steaks on top of one another. Simmer in hot, but not boiling water in a covered pan. Add one-half teaspoon salt and one tablespoon vinegar or lemon juice for each four cups of water. Simmer at the rate of fifteen minutes per pound of fish. Drain and serve with white sauce. Poach in bouillon if desired.

Pan-frying: Pan frying is a term applied to cooking in a small amount of fat in a fry pan. When well controlled, it is an excellent way of cooking pan-dressed fish, fillets, and steaks. Usually you begin by dipping the fish in a liquid and then coating them with a breading. Heat about one-eighth inch of fat in the bottom of a heavy fry pan heated to 350 degrees. Place one layer of breaded fish in the hot fat, taking care not to overload the pan and thus cool the fat. Fry until brown on one side, then turn and brown the other side. Cooking time depends on the thickness of the fish. In general allow about eight to ten minutes. Drain oil from fish after frying.

Steaming: Wrap fish as for poaching. Place on a rack above boiling water. Do not put the fish in the water. Cover tightly and steam for about twelve to fifteen minutes per pound. Add seasoning after the fish has been removed from the steamer. Use about one-half teaspoon of salt and one-eighth teaspoon pepper per pound of fish.

Baking: This is the most common method of preparing fish. Fish may be baked with or without stuffing. Dry the cleaned fish and sprinkle lightly inside and out with salt and pepper, allowing about one-half teaspoon of salt per pound of fish, and one-eighth teaspoon of pepper. Rub fish with oil, butter or margarine, or use strips of bacon placed over the fish. Place in greased pan, uncovered, and bake in a moderately hot oven (400 degrees) at the rate of ten minutes per pound for unstuffed fish and fifteen to twenty minutes per pound for stuffed. Fish should be nicely browned and loose under the skin when done. Remove to a platter and garnish with lemon slices and sprigs of parsley.

Cooking fish for salads: *Boiling water method* — Place a piece of fish on a greased piece of aluminum foil. Season with salt and pepper. Wrap fish in foil, make a double fold on the top and sides, and pinch the foil to make it watertight. Cook in boiling water. Cover the container and when the water returns to the boil, time the cooking period. Allow ten minutes for each one-inch thickness of fish if fresh. If frozen allow twenty minutes. Chill when done and flake for salads. *Steaming method* — Prepare in aluminum foil as for cooking in boiling water. Instead of placing the packet in water, bake in a very hot oven (450 to 500 degrees) in a shallow pan. Allow fifteen minutes cooking time for each one-inch thickness of fresh fish or twenty-five minutes for frozen fish. Chill and flake.

Appetizers

Tantalizing Tartar

Fresh salmon 4 pounds
Lemons 2
Onion 1, minced
Tabasco sauce 1 drop
Garlic clove 1 (optional)
Imported mustard 1 tablespoon
Parsley ½ cup finely minced
Dillweed 1 tablespoon
Brandy 2 tablespoons
Salt to taste
Pepper to taste
Parsley garnish
Citrus garnish
Fresh vegetables garnish
Toast triangles

Skin and debone salmon. Using a chopping cleaver, chop salmon until it is in tiny pieces; place in a glass bowl and set aside. Squeeze lemons over salmon and set aside. Add next 9 ingredients; mix thoroughly. Refrigerate for about 3 hours. Turn into a decorated bowl or mold for shape. Turn mold onto a plate for serving. Garnish salmon with parsley, citrus, and vegetables alternated with toast triangles. Serve with a dry white wine. Serves 8.

Salmon Fondue

Salmon   1 7¾-ounce can
Salmon liquid   ¼ cup
Bread slices   5
Milk   1 cup
Butter   3 tablespoons
Eggs   3, separated
Salt   ½ teaspoon
Cayenne   dash
Mild cheese   ½ cup grated

Preheat oven to 350°. Drain and flake salmon; remove skin and bones; reserve liquid. Trim crusts from bread and cut slices into ½-inch cubes. Heat milk, butter, bread, and liquid from salmon in double boiler. Beat egg yolks; add salt and cayenne; gradually pour in the milk mixture, stirring constantly. Return mixture to double boiler and cook until it thickens. Remove from heat; stir in cheese. Correct seasoning. Cook and stir in salmon. Whip egg whites until stiff; fold into mixture. Pour into a well-buttered baking dish and place dish in a shallow pan of hot water. Bake for 1 hour, or until a knife inserted comes out clean. Serves 6.

Crunchy Canapés

Bread slices 12, toasted
Salmon 1 7¾-ounce can
Mayonnaise ⅓ cup
Ripe olives 2 tablespoons chopped
Parsley 1 tablespoon chopped
Onion 1 teaspoon finely chopped
Mustard 1 teaspoon
Worcestershire sauce ¼ teaspoon

Cut each slice of bread twice diagonally, forming 4 triangles. Drain and flake salmon; remove skin and bones. Combine all ingredients except bread. Spread about 1 teaspoon of mixture on each triangle. Broil 4 inches from heat until mixture has slightly bubbled or about 1 minute. Makes 48.

Smoked Salmon Canapés

Smoked salmon 1 7¾-ounce can
Mayonnaise ¼ cup
Lemon juice 1 tablespoon
Horseradish 1 teaspoon
Onion 1 teaspoon minced
Liquid smoke ¼ teaspoon
Pastry for 1 9-inch pie
Paprika dash

Preheat oven to 450°. Drain and flake salmon; remove skin and bones. Add next 5 ingredients; mix thoroughly. Divide pastry into 2 parts. Roll very thin in circles about 9 inches in diameter. Spread each circle with ½ cup salmon mixture. Cut into 16 wedge-shaped pieces; begin at round edge and roll toward center. Place rolls on a baking pan; prick top of each canapé to allow steam to escape. Sprinkle with paprika. Bake for 10 to 15 minutes or until lightly browned. Makes 32.

Cheese Flips

Salmon   1 15½-ounce can
Bacon strips   4
Condensed cream of cheese soup   ¾ cup
Horseradish   1 teaspoon
Onion   1 teaspoon minced
Salt   to taste
Pepper   to taste
Cheese canapé pastry   your favorite recipe, enough for
    a 2-crust 9-inch pie

Preheat oven to 350°. Drain and flake salmon; remove skin and bones. Fry bacon until crisp; drain and crumble. Combine all ingredients except pastry; set aside. Roll pastry very thin and cut in 2½-inch squares. Place a heaping teaspoon of salmon mixture on ½ of each square. Fold over and press edges together with a fork. Place turnovers on baking pan; prick the top of each turnover to allow steam to escape. Bake for 10 to 15 minutes, or until lightly browned. Makes 80.

Sherry Spread

Salmon 1 7¾-ounce can
Sherry 2 tablespoons
Oil 1 tablespoon
Soy sauce dash
Green onion 1 tablespoon chopped
Pimiento 1 tablespoon chopped
Seasoning salt to taste
Tomatoes garnish
Cucumbers garnish
Rye or pumpernickel bread

Drain and flake salmon; remove skin and bones. Add next 6 ingredients to salmon and chill for 2 hours. Serve with sliced tomatoes, cucumbers, and buttered rye bread. Makes 1 cup.

Jerry's Avocado Spread

Salmon 1 7¾-ounce can
Avocado 1
Lemon juice 1 tablespoon
Oil 1 tablespoon
Garlic clove 1, minced
Onion 2 tablespoons grated
Salt ½ teaspoon
Tabasco sauce 4 drops
Crackers

Drain and flake salmon; remove skin and bones. Mash avocado and combine all ingredients except crackers with salmon. Chill until ready to serve. Serve on crackers. Makes about 2 cups; serves 6.

Creamy Smoked Salmon Roll

Unflavored gelatin   1½ teaspoons
Cold water   6 tablespoons
Heavy cream   ½ cup
Horseradish   2 tablespoons, drained
Lemon juice   1 teaspoon
Sugar   ½ teaspoon
Smoked salmon   ¾ pound, thinly sliced
Pumpernickel bread   thinly sliced
Lemon   cut into wedges
Lettuce   garnish
Freshly ground pepper   to taste

Sprinkle gelatin over cold water in a small saucepan; stir over low heat until dissolved; let mixture cool slightly and chill for 5 minutes. Whip the cream; stir in horseradish, lemon juice, and sugar. Add to gelatin mixture. Beat until mixture is quite thick; chill for 5 minutes. Place a generous spoonful of mixture down the center of each salmon piece. Fold the 2 sides over so that they overlap slightly. Place each salmon roll seam side down on a baking sheet lined with waxed paper; place plastic wrap on top and chill. Garnish with pumpernickel bread, lemon, lettuce, and pepper. Serves 6.

Curried Eggs

Salmon 1 15½-ounce can
Mayonnaise ⅔ cup
Chili sauce 1 tablespoon
Pimiento 1 teaspoon chopped
Green pepper 1 tablespoon chopped
Onion 1 teaspoon grated
Curry powder ¼ teaspoon
Eggs 18, hard-cooked
Mayonnaise 2 tablespoons
Salt to taste
Pepper to taste
Mustard ⅛ teaspoon
Parsley garnish
Lemon juice garnish

Drain, remove skin and bones, and mash salmon. Add mayonnaise, chili sauce, pimiento, green pepper, onion, and curry powder. Blend and chill. Cut eggs in half lengthwise and remove yolks. Place salmon mixture in egg whites. Mash egg yolks and mix in a little mayonnaise, salt, pepper, and mustard; place on top of salmon mixture. Garnish with parsley and a squeeze of lemon juice. Makes 36.

Nutty Party Ball

Salmon   1 15½-ounce can
Cream cheese   8 ounces, softened
Lemon juice   1 tablespoon
Salt   ¼ teaspoon
Onion   2 teaspoons grated
Horseradish   1 teaspoon
Liquid smoke   ¼ teaspoon
Pecans   ½ cup chopped (optional)
Parsley   3 tablespoons chopped
Crackers or flatbread

Drain and flake salmon; remove bones and skin. Combine next 6 ingredients with salmon; mix thoroughly; chill for 3 hours. Combine pecans and parsley. Shape salmon mixture into a ball then roll in nut mixture. Chill for 15 minutes, and serve with crackers. Makes 3 cups.

Smoked Salmon Dip
with Sour Cream

Smoked salmon   2 cups crumbled
Sour cream   1 cup
Garlic salt   to taste
Dillweed   to taste
Chips, crackers, or flatbread

Mix first 4 ingredients together. Refrigerate for 1 hour. Serve with chips. Makes 2 cups.

Red Caviar Cream Dip

Salmon   1 15 ½-ounce can
Salt   ½ teaspoon
Tabasco sauce   2 drops
Onion   1 teaspoon grated
Sour cream   1 cup
Radishes   2, thinly sliced
Red caviar   1 tablespoon, drained (optional)
Crackers or flatbread

Drain, remove skin and bones, and mash salmon. Blend in salt, tabasco, and onion; mix with sour cream. Chill for about 30 minutes. Slice radishes and add to mixture just before serving. Mix caviar into dip or place on top of dip. Serve with crackers. Makes 2 cups.

Speedy Smoked Dip with Capers

Smoked salmon   ½ cup
Heavy cream   ⅓ cup
Capers   ½ teaspoon (optional)
Pepper   ⅛ teaspoon
Toast triangles or chips

Using an electric blender, combine first 4 ingredients and blend until smooth. If you do not have a blender, grind the salmon and capers, whip the cream, and combine all ingredients. Serve with toast triangles. Makes ¾ cup.

Soups
and
Chowders

Salmon Court Bouillon

Water   1 quart
Sauterne or white wine   ½ gallon
Onion   1
Parsley sprigs   7 or 8
Thyme   dash
Bay leaf   1
Seasoning salt   1 teaspoon
Peppercorns   8 to 10
Salmon   1 2-pound piece
White sauce   your favorite recipe*

Combine first 8 ingredients in large saucepan or kettle; simmer for 45 minutes. Cool broth completely; strain through sieve. Place salmon on rack in cold prepared broth (court bouillon). Very slowly bring liquid to simmering (it will take about 30 minutes). Simmer 25 minutes. When cooked, peel off skin. Serve hot with white sauce. Serves 4 to 6.
*If desired, use part of the cooking broth as sauce liquid.

Note: If you serve the salmon cold, decorate with anchovy fillets, sliced pickles, sliced hard-cooked eggs, and a green sauce (thinned mayonnaise with chopped parsley and chopped tarragon leaves added).

Bristol Bisque

Salmon 1 15½-ounce can
Butter or margarine ¼ cup, melted
Celery ¼ cup chopped
Onion ¼ cup chopped
Flour 3 tablespoons
Salmon liquid and milk 3 cups combined
Tomato juice 1 cup
Salt 1½ tablespoons
Parsley 1 tablespoon chopped
Crackers

Drain salmon, reserving liquid; remove skin and bones, and flake. Place butter, celery, and onion in a pan over low heat; cook until tender. Stir in flour and gradually add salmon liquid and milk; cook and stir over low heat until slightly thickened. Blend in tomato juice; add salt, parsley, and salmon. Heat thoroughly but do not boil. Serve piping hot with crackers. Serves 6.

Londoner's Soup

Salmon head   1
Salmon tail or small salmon steak   1
Halibut head   1
Sole   skeletons from filleting
Leek   1, chopped
Carrots   2, chopped
Celery   1 small piece, chopped
Large onion   1, chopped
Garlic clove   1, halved
Salt   1 tablespoon
Peppercorns   12
Parsley stalks   1 bunch
Lemon thyme sprig   1
Tarragon   to taste
Bay leaf   1
Lemon rind   1 thinly peeled
Paprika   2 teaspoons
Fennel seeds   12
Juniper berries   6
Coriander seeds   12 lightly crushed
Cold water   3 pints
Tomatoes   4, halved, lightly grilled, and skinned
Parmesan cheese   2 teaspoons grated
Nutmeg   ½ teaspoon freshly grated
Salt   to taste
Pepper   to taste
Medium sherry   1 tablespoon and/or
      Flaming brandy   2 tablespoons
Heavy cream   4 or 5 tablespoons

Put the salmon head and tail, halibut head, and sole skeletons into a large saucepan with the leek, carrots, celery, onion, garlic, salt, peppercorns, herbs, and spices.* Cover with a good 3 pints of cold water and bring to a boil. After about 25 minutes add tomatoes. Simmer for a total of 35 to 40 minutes. Flake the flesh from salmon head. Put about ½ pint of stock into an electric blender together with the flaked salmon, tomatoes, some of the carrot, onion, and other seasonings, and blend to a smooth cream. (Or, you can put this mixture through a vegetable mill and press through a sieve.) Return to the pan with rest of stock and reheat, adding the cheese and nutmeg, and more salt and pepper. If too thin, simmer soup until it has reduced a little; if too thick, dilute with a little white wine. If it does not taste salmony enough to you, add about 2 ounces canned salmon blended with a little cream or milk. Finally, stir in the sherry and/or brandy and add the cream just before serving. Serves 4.

*Do not worry if you cannot find fennel seeds, juniper berries, or coriander seeds as they are not absolutely essential.

Note: This is a sensationally good soup — an ideal dish with which to begin a dinner party. If served with slices of French bread rubbed with garlic and dried in the oven, it makes quite a substantial family meal.

Hearty Alaskan Salmon Chowder

Salmon   8 15½-ounce cans
Salmon liquid and water   1½ gallons combined
Onions   1¼ quarts chopped
Butter or margarine   1 cup, melted
Condensed cream of mushroom soup   22 pounds (2½ gallons)
Milk   1½ gallons
Large potatoes   6, peeled and shredded
Parsley   2½ cups chopped
Salt   4 tablespoons
White pepper   1 teaspoon

Drain salmon, reserving liquid to use with water; remove skin and bones; flake salmon. Sauté onions in butter until clear in appearance, not browned. In a large kettle, add soup, milk, and salmon liquid and water; mix well. Add salmon, potatoes, and onions; include pan drippings. Heat to a medium-hot temperature. Add parsley, salt, and pepper; let chowder cook for 1 hour. Serves 100.

Note: This recipe is versatile. Add chopped celery, mushrooms, tomatoes, and complementary spices to make this chowder more like a stew-chowder.

Ketchikan Chowder with Milk

Salmon 3 pounds
Water enough to cover fish
Bay leaf 1
Parsley sprig 1
Peppercorns 3
Salt ¼ teaspoon
Large potatoes 3, diced
Salt pork ¼ pound, diced
Large onions 2, sliced
Milk 6 cups
Salt to taste
Pepper to taste

Carefully place salmon in deep pot; cover with water (no more than that amount); add bay leaf, parsley, peppercorns, and salt; boil 15 minutes, or until salmon can be flaked with fork and broth is cooked down. While salmon is cooking, boil potatoes and prepare pork and onions as follows: place pork in skillet; fry over medium flame 15 minutes, or until golden brown and well done; add onions, brown 5 minutes, stirring constantly. Remove cooked salmon and flake in large pieces. Heat deep soup tureen by letting it stand in very hot water. Place salmon, potatoes, onions, and salt pork in heated tureen; cover to keep hot. In a separate pot, heat milk to almost the boiling point; pour milk over hot ingredients; add salt and pepper. Serve piping hot in preheated chowder bowls. Serves 6 to 8.

Potato Chowder, San Juan Style

Salmon 1 15½-ounce can
Water 2 cups
Tomato juice 1 cup
Onion ½ cup chopped
Potatoes 1 cup cubed
Celery salt 1 teaspoon
Butter 4 tablespoons, melted
Flour 4 tablespoons
Salt 1 teaspoon
Dry mustard 1 teaspoon
Worcestershire sauce ½ teaspoon
Milk 3 cups

Drain, flake, and remove skin and bones from salmon. Combine first 6 ingredients in a large kettle; cover and simmer for 40 minutes. In another saucepan melt butter; add flour, salt, mustard, and Worcestershire sauce; mix until smooth. Add milk slowly and stir constantly; cook until mixture thickens; combine with salmon mix. Stir well and serve hot. Serves 8.

Pier 89 Salmon Chowder

Salmon   2 cups cooked and flaked or 1 15½-ounce can
Chicken bouillon   1 cube
Water   1 cup, boiling
Butter, margarine, or bacon fat   ¼ cup
Onion   ½ cup chopped
Green pepper   ¼ cup chopped
Tomatoes   1 16-ounce can
Whole-kernel corn   1 8-ounce can
Salt   ½ teaspoon
Pepper   dash
Thyme   ¼ teaspoon

If using canned salmon, drain, remove skin and bones, and break up into chunks. Dissolve bouillon in boiling water. In a small skillet, melt butter and cook onion and green pepper until tender; use low heat. Combine all ingredients. Cook for approximately 15 minutes to blend flavors. Serves 4 to 6.

Baton Rouge Salmon Chowder

Salmon   1 15½-ounce can
Chicken bouillon   1 cube
Water   1 cup, boiling
Onion   ¾ cup chopped
Green pepper   ½ cup finely chopped
Garlic clove   1, finely chopped
Butter or other fat   ¼ cup, melted
Salmon liquid   ⅓ cup
Tomatoes   1 16-ounce can
Whole-kernel corn   1 8-ounce can
Okra   1 cup sliced (optional)
Salt   ½ teaspoon
Thyme   ¼ teaspoon
Pepper   dash
Bay leaf   1

Drain salmon, remove skin and bones, and reserve liquid; break salmon into large pieces. Dissolve bouillon in water. Cook onion, green pepper, and garlic in butter until tender. Combine all ingredients including salmon liquid and cook for 15 minutes or until vegetables are tender. Remove bay leaf before serving. Serves 6.

Fisherman's Salmon Chowder

Salmon   1 15½-ounce can
Salmon liquid and milk   2¾ cups combined
Butter or margarine   ¼ cup, melted
Onion   ¼ cup chopped
Flour   3 tablespoons
Salt   ½ teaspoon
Pepper   dash
Bay leaf   1
Medium potatoes   2, peeled, cooked, and cubed
Parsley   1 tablespoon

Drain salmon, remove skin and bones, and reserve liquid; break into chunks. Add milk to salmon liquid to equal 2¾ cups. In a 3-quart saucepan melt butter and sauté onion; blend in flour, salt, and pepper; add milk/salmon liquid mixture and bay leaf. Cook and stir until thickened and bubbly. Add salmon chunks, potatoes, and parsley. Heat through. Serves 4.

Salads

Salmon Louis

Salmon   1 15½-ounce can
Head of lettuce   1
Tomatoes   2, cut into sixths
Louis Dressing   1 cup
Egg yolks   2, hard-cooked and sieved

Drain and flake salmon; remove bones and skin. Shred lettuce and place in shallow salad bowl. Arrange salmon over lettuce; place tomatoes around the edge. Serve with Louis Dressing and egg yolks. Serves 6.

Louis Dressing

Mayonnaise   ½ cup
Whipping cream   2 tablespoons
Chili sauce   2 tablespoons
Green pepper   2 tablespoons chopped
Green onions   2 tablespoons chopped
Egg whites   2 hard-cooked and chopped
Olives   1 tablespoon chopped
Lemon juice   ½ teaspoon
Salt   dash
Pepper   dash

Combine all ingredients and chill. Makes 1 cup.

Cold Salmon with Cucumber Dressing

Salmon 1 15½-ounce can
Medium cucumbers 2
Lemon juice 2 tablespoons
Plain yogurt 1 cup
Watercress or lettuce garnish

Chill salmon. Remove carefully from can, drain, and discard any skin and bones; arrange large chunks on 3 plates. Peel and seed cucumbers; dice and sprinkle with lemon juice; let stand 15 minutes. Drain and combine with yogurt. Spread over salmon, and garnish plates generously with watercress. Serves 3.

Note: As canned salmon is often salty, the cucumber-yogurt sauce is deliberately left unsalted. Each serving is less than 300 calories.

Dieter's Cabbage Salad

Cabbage 4 cups shredded
Mayonnaise ¾ cup
Dry mustard ½ teaspoon
Parsley 1 tablespoon chopped
Tarragon ¼ teaspoon
Garlic clove ½, crushed
Dillweed ½ teaspoon
Onion 1 or 2 tablespoons finely chopped
Eggs 3, hard-cooked
Salmon 2 15½-ounce cans
Lettuce garnish
Ripe olives ½ cup sliced
Tomato cut into wedges

Shred cabbage. Make dressing by combining the mayonnaise, seasonings, and 2 chopped eggs. Blend well. Add dressing to cabbage and mix together. Drain and remove salmon's skin and bones; break into pieces; add to salad and toss together. Place on lettuce. Serve with sliced hard-cooked egg, olives, and tomato. Serves 6.

Fresh Fruit Salad Tosser

Salmon 1 15½-ounce can
Lemon juice 1 tablespoon
Oranges 2, cut into chunks
Banana 1, sliced
Apple 1, diced but unpeeled
Mayonnaise ¼ cup
Lettuce 3 cups torn
Almonds ¼ cup blanched and toasted

Drain, remove skin and bones, and sprinkle bite-sized salmon chunks with lemon juice. Lightly toss with next 4 ingredients. Serve at once in lettuce cups. Top with almonds. Serves 6.

Apple Surprise Salad

Lemon juice 1 tablespoon
Red apple 1 cup diced
Salmon 1 15½-ounce can
Celery 1 cup chopped
Salted peanuts ½ cup
Mayonnaise ½ cup
Lettuce garnish

Sprinkle lemon juice over apple. Combine with drained, deboned, and skinned salmon chunks; add next 3 ingredients. Toss lightly and serve in lettuce cups. Serves 4.

Smoked Dinner Salad

Mayonnaise   1 cup
Prepared mustard   1 teaspoon
Tarragon leaves   ½ teaspoon
Salt   ½ teaspoon
Celery seed   ¼ teaspoon
Potatoes   3 cups cooked, sliced, and chilled
Celery   2 cups sliced
Radishes   ⅔ cup sliced
Green onions   ⅓ cup sliced
Smoked salmon   ½ pound, flaked
Lettuce   garnish
Vegetables   garnish

Combine first 5 ingredients; mix well. Fold in potatoes. Cover; refrigerate several hours to blend flavors. Add celery, radishes, onion, and fish; mix carefully. Arrange in center of lettuce-lined serving dish. To garnish, place additional sliced salmon around salad with fresh, crisp, cut vegetables. Serves 6.

Almond and Avocado Mounds

Salmon 1 15½-ounce can
Avocado 1, peeled and sliced
Lemon juice 1 tablespoon
Orange sections 2 cups
Celery 1½ cups sliced
Slivered almonds ½ cup blanched
Mayonnaise ⅓ cup
Salad greens garnish

Drain and remove skin and bones from salmon; break into large pieces. Sprinkle avocado with lemon juice to prevent discoloration. Reserve 6 avocado slices and 6 orange sections for garnish. Cut remaining avocado and orange into 1-inch pieces. Combine all ingredients except salad greens; chill. Shape into a mound on salad greens and garnish with alternate slices of avocado and orange. Serves 6.

Maui Salmon Platter

Salmon   2 cups chunks
Small pineapple   1*
Avocado   1
Lemon juice   from 1 lemon
Papaya   1
Mandarin oranges   2 11-ounce cans
Sour cream   1 cup
Lime   1, juice and gratings
Chutney   1 cup finely chopped
Macadamia nuts   1 cup chopped

On a large tray, about 12 x 18 inches, arrange salmon in center in 1 row. Peel pineapple, remove eyes, and slice into rounds; halve the slices and remove core; arrange a row of pineapple down the left side. Halve, peel, and slice avocado; dip each slice into lemon juice. Peel, halve, remove seeds, and slice papaya. Drain mandarin oranges. Arrange papaya in a row on the right side of salmon. Arrange slices of avocado, and mandarin oranges. Cover and chill. Mix sour cream with juice of a lime and grated peel; add chopped chutney; chill. Serve dressing topped with nuts in small separate bowls at serving time. Serves 6.
*Canned pineapple may be substituted.

Salmon Cabbage Vinaigrette

Salmon   1 15½-ounce can
Raw cabbage   4 cups shredded
Onion   ¼ cup chopped
Parlsley   ¼ cup chopped
Eggs   2, hard-cooked and chopped
Vinaigrette Dressing
Large cabbage leaves   18

Drain, remove skin and bones, and flake salmon. Combine cabbage, onion, parsley, eggs, and salmon. Add Vinaigrette Dressing and mix thoroughly. Serve in the center of a cabbage rosette; chill. Serves 6.

Vinaigrette Dressing

Salt   1 teaspoon
Cayenne   dash
Paprika   ¼ teaspoon
Vinegar   3 tablespoons
Olive or salad oil   ½ cup
Pimiento   1 tablespoon chopped
Sweet pickle   1 tablespoon chopped
Green pepper   1 tablespoon chopped

Combine salt, cayenne, and paprika. Add vinegar and oil slowly, beating thoroughly. Add pimiento, pickle, and green pepper; mix well.

Simple Salmon Tosser

Salmon 1 15½-ounce can
Lemon juice 2 tablespoons
Mayonnaise ½ cup
Prepared horseradish 1 teaspoon
Salt dash
Cayenne dash
Celery ⅔ cup diced
Stuffed olives ¼ cup sliced
Chives 2 tablespoons chopped
Eggs 2, hard-cooked and chopped
Lettuce garnish
Paprika garnish

Drain salmon, remove skin and bones, and flake; sprinkle with lemon juice. In a large mixing bowl blend mayonnaise and horseradish; add salt and cayenne. Mix celery, olives, 1 tablespoon chives, and eggs with mayonnaise mixture; add salmon carefully. Serve on crisp lettuce leaves on a prechilled salad plate. Sprinkle with paprika and remaining chopped chives. Serves 4 to 6.

Salmon Buffet Bowl

Salmon 1 15½-ounce can
Mayonnaise 1 cup
Chili sauce ¼ cup
Green pepper ¼ cup finely chopped
Green onion ¼ cup finely chopped
Lemon juice 1 teaspoon
Whipping cream ½ cup
Large head of romaine 1
Tomatoes 2, cut into wedges
Eggs 2, hard-cooked and sliced lengthwise
Parsley garnish

Drain salmon, remove skin and bones, and break into chunks; chill. Blend together mayonnaise, chili sauce, green pepper, green onion, and lemon juice; chill. At serving time, whip cream just until soft peaks form; fold into mayonnaise mixture. Line salad bowl with outer leaves of romaine; tear up remaining romaine and place in bowl; place salmon chunks across center of lettuce. Surround salmon with tomatoes and eggs. Garnish with parsley. Serve dressing in small bowl. Serves 4.

Skillet Salad

Salad oil   2 tablespoons
Flour   1 tablespoon
Sugar   1 tablespoon
Onion   1 tablespoon minced
Garlic salt   1 teaspoon
Dry mustard   ½ teaspoon
Pepper   dash
Water   ½ cup
Vinegar   ¼ cup
Salmon   1 15½-ounce can
Eggs   3, hard-cooked and sliced
Celery   ½ cup sliced
Lettuce   3 cups torn
Cucumber   ½ cup unpeeled and thinly sliced
Large tomato   cut into wedges

In medium skillet blend first 7 ingredients. Add water and vinegar; cook over medium heat until mixture boils, stirring constantly. Drain salmon, remove skin and bones, and break into chunks. In the hot sauce layer in order: salmon, eggs, celery, lettuce, cucumber, and tomato. Cook, covered, over medium heat until heated through (about 4 to 5 minutes). Remove from heat and toss together lightly. Serves 4.

Lomi Lomi Stuffed Tomatoes

Salmon   1 7¾-ounce can
Celery   ½ cup chopped
Mayonnaise   ¼ cup
Onion   1 tablespoon finely chopped
Sweet pickle   1 tablespoon chopped
Egg   1, hard-cooked and chopped
Medium tomatoes   6
Lettuce   garnish

Drain, remove skin and bones, and flake salmon; combine with next 5 ingredients. Wash tomatoes, cut off tops, and scoop out part of centers. Spoon in salmon filling, piling it high. Serve on a leaf of lettuce. Serves 6.

Potpourri Macaroni Salad

Macaroni   1 8-ounce package
Salmon   1 15½-ounce can
Onion   2 tablespoons finely chopped
Celery   4 tablespoons chopped
Parsley   2 tablespoons chopped
Medium cucumber   1, sliced
Salt   1 teaspoon
Salad dressing   ½ cup
Salad greens   garnish
Egg   1, hard-cooked
Black olives   6, sliced

Cook macaroni according to directions on package. Drain and rinse with cold water. Drain and remove skin and bones from salmon; combine with onion, celery, parsley, cucumber, salt, and salad dressing. Add to macaroni, mix well. Line large salad bowl with salad greens. Pour in macaroni mixture. Garnish with egg slices and rings of sliced olives. Chill. Serves 6.

Quick 'n' Easy Salmon Mold

Sugar ¼ cup
Unflavored gelatin 1 envelope
Salt ¼ teaspoon
Water 1¼ cups
Vinegar ¼ cup
Lemon juice 1 tablespoon
Cucumber 1 cup peeled and diced
Celery ½ cup diced
Salmon 1 15½-ounce can
Salmon liquid and water ½ cup combined
Unflavored gelatin 1 envelope
Water ¼ cup
Mayonnaise ½ cup
Lemon juice 1 teaspoon
Lettuce garnish

In a saucepan, combine sugar, 1 envelope gelatin, and salt; stir in 1¼ cups water, vinegar, and 1 tablespoon lemon juice. Cook and stir until mixture boils and gelatin is dissolved. Remove from heat and chill until partially set. Fold in cucumber and celery; turn into a 5-cup mold. Chill until almost set. Drain, flake, and remove skin and bones from salmon; reserve liquid; add enough water to liquid to make ½ cup. Set aside. Soften 1 envelope gelatin in ¼ cup water; dissolve over hot water. Combine mayonnaise, reserved salmon liquid and water, and 1 teaspoon lemon juice. Stir in salmon; blend in dissolved gelatin, and spoon over cucumber layer. Chill until firm. Unmold and garnish with lettuce. Serves 6.

Sour Cream and Lemon Mold

Unflavored gelatin   1 envelope
Cold water   ½ cup
Sour cream sauce mix   1 envelope
Mayonnaise   ½ cup
Lemon juice   2 teaspoons
Dillweed   ¼ teaspoon
Salmon   1 15½-ounce can
Celery   ½ cup diced

Soften gelatin in water; stir over low heat until gelatin dissolves; let cool. Prepare sour cream sauce mix according to package directions. Blend in mayonnaise, lemon juice, and dillweed. Gradually stir in gelatin. Drain salmon, discarding skin and large bones; flake. Fold salmon and celery into sour cream mixture. Turn into a 3½-cup mold; chill until firm; unmold. Serves 4.

Supreme Supper Salad

Salmon 1 15½-ounce can
Potatoes 6 cups diced and cooked
Celery 1½ cups minced
Cucumber 1 cup diced
Green onions ½ cup sliced
Fresh basil 1 tablespoon chopped
Mayonnaise 1½ cups
Sour cream ½ cup
Pepper ¼ teaspoon
Salt 1 teaspoon
Lemon juice or vinegar 2 tablespoons
Parsley garnish
Mayonnaise base dressing your favorite kind

Drain and flake salmon; remove skin and bones. Combine salmon with potatoes, celery, cucumber, onions, and basil. Combine mayonnaise, sour cream, pepper, salt, and lemon juice. Stir into potato-salmon mixture. Pack into a 10-cup mold and chill. When ready to serve, unmold onto cold serving platter and garnish with parsley. Serve with dressing. Serves 6.

Entrées

Baked Salmon with Herb Butter

Salmon fillet   2 to 2½ pounds
Butter or margarine   ¼ cup
Garlic clove   1, minced or mashed
Small onion   1, finely chopped
Parsley   3 tablespoons minced
Lemon juice   2 tablespoons
Sweet basil   ½ teaspoon crumbled
Salt   1 teaspoon
Freshly ground pepper   ½ teaspoon

Preheat oven to 300°. Place salmon fillet on a piece of heavy paper or foil, and cut around fish (paper keeps salmon skin from sticking to rack); slide fish and paper onto rack of broiler pan. Blend together remaining ingredients; spread over fillet. Bake for 25 to 30 minutes, depending on thickness of fillet, or until fish flakes with a fork. Serves 8.

Note: Mrs. Jon Lindbergh simplifies my recipe. She heats the sauce, spreads it over the salmon, and bakes the salmon for only 15 to 25 minutes depending on thickness of fish. And she doubles the sauce and serves some separately with a ladle.

Savory Poached Steaks

Salmon steaks   4, 6 ounces each
Onion   ½, thinly sliced
Carrot   1, sliced
Water   2 cups
Celery stalk   1, chopped
Peppercorns   10
Thyme   ½ teaspoon
Lemon   juice of 1
Salt   pinch

Place cleaned salmon steaks in skillet and add remaining ingredients; liquid should barely cover fish. Simmer covered for 20 minutes. Using slotted spatula, transfer salmon to platter and serve hot. Serves 4.

Fillet au Gratin

Salmon fillets 2 pounds
Salt to taste
Pepper to taste
Lemon juice 3 tablespoons
Butter 1 tablespoon
Creamy Cheese Sauce
Grated cheese 4 tablespoons

Clean fish and sprinkle with salt and pepper. Place in buttered 2-quart casserole, pour lemon juice over fish, dot with butter, and cover with foil. Bake in hot oven (approximately 400°) for 20 minutes. Pour off fish stock and save. Prepare Creamy Cheese Sauce. Pour sauce over fish, sprinkle with grated cheese, and brown under broiler additional 10 minutes. Serves 6 to 8.

Creamy Cheese Sauce

Butter 2 tablespoons, melted
Flour 3 tablespoons
Fish stock and cream 1½ cups combined
Egg yolks 2
Butter 2 tablespoons
Grated cheese 2 tablespoons
Salt to taste
Pepper to taste

Melt butter; add flour and blend well. Add stock and cream; simmer for 10 minutes over low heat. Remove from heat; add egg yolks, butter, and cheese, stirring until smooth. Season to taste. Makes about 2 cups.

Hickory-Broiled Salmon Steaks

Hickory Sauce

Catsup ½ cup
Salad oil ¼ cup
Lemon juice 3 tablespoons
Vinegar 2 tablespoons
Hickory liquid smoke 1 tablespoon
Worcestershire sauce 1 teaspoon
Salt 1 teaspoon
Tabasco sauce 3 drops
Powdered mustard 1 teaspoon
Celery salt ¼ teaspoon
Soy sauce 1 tablespoon
Garlic clove 1, chopped

Combine all ingredients and mix well. Makes about 1½ cups.

Salmon steaks 6, 6 to 8 ounces each
Salt 2 tablespoons
Water 1 cup

Place salmon in a shallow pan. Mix salt and water and pour over steaks; soak in salt solution for 3 minutes. Place steaks in clean pan. Pour sauce over steaks; marinate for 30 minutes. Charcoal broil or oven broil steaks 8 to 10 minutes, or until fish is lightly browned on 1 side; baste with sauce. Turn steak and broil 5 minutes longer or until flesh flakes easily; baste with sauce. Serve remaining marinade sauce with steaks. Serves 6.

Novotny's Bohemian Barbecued Salmon

Mr. Novotny is one of the "fathers" of pan-sized salmon. He started raising the fish in open sea net pens in Puget Sound, Washington, in 1969.

Salt 1 teaspoon
Ground pepper ½ teaspoon
Salmon fillets 2 pounds
Onion salt to taste
Garlic salt to taste
Butter ⅔ cup, melted
Kikkoman Memmi Soup Base 3 tablespoons
Parlsey garnish
Dill seed garnish
Fresh mushrooms (optional)

Rub salt and pepper into salmon, sprinkle *lightly* with onion salt and garlic salt. Make a container from aluminum foil, or place fillets skin side down in an aluminum tray. In a small saucepan, heat butter until melted; add soup base; brush this hot mixture liberally over the fillets and allow them to marinate for 15 minutes. Broil or barbecue, basting occasionally. Just before fillets are cooked, baste once more and sprinkle with parsley and a small amount of dill seed. Finish cooking and serve. After garnishing fillets with parsley and dill seed, sliced mushrooms may be put on top of each fillet prior to final basting. Serves 4.

Note: This recipe is especially well suited for salmon from pan-sized to 3 to 4 pounds, but can be used for any size fish. For larger fish, an appetizing fillet can be prepared by removing all fins and bones with a quality fillet knife. Larger boned fillets can be placed directly on a barbecue grill and basted frequently with the sauce until done.

Sesame Salmon Barbeque

Salmon steaks   4, 6 to 8 ounces each (1-inch thick)
Vegetable oil   2 tablespoons
Sesame seeds   2 tablespoons
Tomato cheese sauce   1 8-ounce can
Brown sugar   1½ tablespoons
Lemon   juice of 1
Oregano   ½ teaspoon
Worcestershire sauce   1 teaspoon
Dry mustard   ¼ teaspoon
Parsley   1 tablespoon finely chopped

Brush salmon steaks with oil and sprinkle with sesame seeds. Combine all other ingredients except parsley in a saucepan and simmer gently for 10 minutes. Place steaks on a hot grill, 2 to 3 inches from glowing coals; baste frequently with sauce. Cook about 15 minutes. Carefully turn steaks to brown both sides. Add parsley to remaining sauce and serve with salmon. Serves 4.

Salmon California

Salmon   1 2- to 3-pound dressed
Lime or lemon juice   ¼ cup
Soy sauce   ¼ cup
Rosé wine   ½ cup
Salad oil   ¼ cup
Parsley sprigs   fresh
Lime or lemon   slices

Cut shallow gashes along back or sides of fish; brush inside cavity with some of the lime juice and soy sauce. Combine remaining lime juice and soy sauce with wine and oil. Tuck parsley sprigs inside of salmon. Place fish in folding wire rack or on grill and brush with oil mixture. Grill for 6 to 8 minutes over charcoal (about 6 inches from heat), brushing often with marinade; carefully turn fish. Continue grilling until fish is done (about 10 minutes longer). Replace parsley inside cavity with fresh sprigs. Serve with slices of lime. Serves 4 to 5.

Grilled Salmon from Peter's Place

Salmon steaks   6, 6-ounces each
Dry vermouth   1 cup
Butter   ⅔ cup, melted
Lemon juice   ¼ cup
Onion   2 tablespoons finely chopped
Salt   2 teaspoons
Marjoram   ¼ teaspoon
Pepper   ¼ teaspoon
Thyme   ¼ teaspoon
Garlic clove   1
Sage   pinch

Place salmon steaks in a single layer in a shallow pan. Combine all other ingredients. Pour sauce over salmon and allow to marinate for 4 hours; turn steaks occasionally. Remove steaks, saving the sauce. Place steaks in a wire grill or basket or place them on grill 4 inches from hot coals for 8 minutes. Turn and cook other side, basting with sauce while steaks are cooking. Serves 6.

Salmon Rosé

Salmon steaks   4, 6 ounces each
Rosé wine   ½ cup
Marjoram   ¼ teaspoon
Onion powder   ½ teaspoon
Pepper   ¹⁄₁₆ teaspoon
Seasoning salt   to taste

Place salmon in shallow pan. Combine wine, marjoram, onion powder, and pepper; pour over fish. Refrigerate for several hours, turning salmon once or twice. Drain well. Grill or broil until fish flakes easily with a fork, turning once; sprinkle with seasoning salt as salmon broils. Serves 4.

Tyee Salmon Steaks

Salmon steaks 6, 6 ounces each
Salad oil ½ cup
Parsley ¼ cup
Lemon juice ¼ cup
Onion 2 tablespoons grated
Dry mustard ½ teaspoon
Salt ¼ teaspoon
Pepper dash

Place salmon in a shallow dish. Combine all other ingredients; pour over fish. Let stand at room temperature 2 hours, turning occasionally (or marinate in refrigerator 4 to 6 hours). Place salmon in well-greased wire broiler basket or on flat rack. Grill over medium-hot coals until lightly browned (6 to 8 minutes); baste with marinade and turn. Brush again with marinade; grill until fish flakes easily when tested with a fork (6 to 8 minutes longer). Serves 6.

Coho Barbecue

Barbecue sauce   ½ cup
Lemon   Juice of 1
Worcestershire sauce   1 tablespoon
Butter   ½ cup
Salmon   1, 6 to 8 pounds

Combine first 4 ingredients and heat until butter is melted. Clean the fish, remove scales, and split along backbone to remove backbone as in filleting. Leave skin on fish. Place fish on well-greased rack; place another well-greased rack of same size on top of salmon. Place on hot barbecue grill 2 to 3 inches above coals. Cook for 10 to 15 minutes with flesh side down, then turn rack over with skin side down and start basting with sauce. Do not overcook; it should done in 25 to 30 minutes. Serves 10 to 12.

Chinook Salmon Barbecue

King salmon   1, 12 to 14 pounds
Salt   to taste
Pepper   to taste
Garlic salt   to taste

Split dressed salmon and remove backbone. Season split sides well with salt, pepper, and garlic salt. Place cut sides down on oiled grill. After fire is hot, put on some green alder; when coals are glowing, place the grill about a foot above coals. Brown cut sides about 20 minutes; turn carefully; let cook 3 to 4 hours. Do not overcook. Serves 12 or more.

Dave Stauer's Salmon with No Longer Secret Barbecue Sauce

According to Jinx Morgan, the Fort Bragg California barbecue is a heck of a bash. Each year, in the eight hours before sundown, about 5,000 souls consume over two tons of prime salmon, 8,000 ears of corn, dozens of buckets of crisp green salad, several truckloads of crusty sourdough French bread, and several acre-feet of beer. The proceeds are donated to the Salmon Restoration Foundation (to help ensure future barbecues!). Here is the "secret" sauce that has guaranteed this event's success.

No Longer Secret Barbecue Sauce

Butter   1 cup, melted
Lemon juice   ⅓ cup
Soy sauce   1½ teaspoons
Worcestershire sauce   1½ teaspoons
Fresh parsley   2 tablespoons
Sweet basil   1 teaspoon
Oregano   1 teaspoon
Garlic powder   ½ teaspoon
Salt   to taste
Pepper   to taste

Salmon steaks or fillets   10 pounds

Combine all sauce ingredients. Rub grill of a barbecue pit or charcoal broiler with cooking oil before placing it over hot coals. Brush salmon steaks or fillets (fillets are better because they have fewer bones) with sauce and broil equally on each side for a total of 10 minutes to the inch of thickness. Brush on more sauce before each turn. Serves 18.

Note: Albeit conceived for salmon, this sauce works well with any fish. You can also dip french bread in it, grill the bread, and then experience a delectable repast.

Ralph Munro's Salmon with Indian Barbecue Sauce

Indian Barbecue Sauce

Butter 2 cups, melted
Brown sugar 2 cups
Salt 2 tablespoons
Pepper 1 teaspoon
Marjoram generous pinch

Fresh salmon 1, 10 pounds
Salt to taste

Combine all sauce ingredients (mix will look like peanut butter). Thoroughly soak salmon with sauce before grilling. Salt flesh side of salmon and place on oiled rack (meat side down) over low fire. Never let a flame hit your fish. Cook slowly for 30 to 40 minutes until skin of fish feels warm. Turn over; baste heavily with sauce; repeat process. Fish is done when meat will peel apart but is still moist. Serves 18.

Note: Do not overcook; make people taste it this way before you serve them lemons, onions, cream sauces, etc. that will alter the taste.

Poached Salmon with Egg Sauce

Salmon   1, 5 to 6 pounds
Water   2½ quarts
Small onion   1, minced
Peppercorns   10
Salt   1 tablespoon
Bouquet garni:
    Whole cloves   ½ teaspoon
    Parsley sprigs   6
    Bay leaves   2
    Thyme sprigs   2
    Celery leaves   4 or
    Lovage leaf   1
Dry white wine   2 cups

In a fish kettle or other pot large enough to hold the whole or piece of salmon, add water, onion, peppercorns, and salt. Tie bouquet garni ingredients in a small cheesecloth bag; add to bouillon, and simmer for 20 minutes. Wipe salmon clean with a cloth and tie firmly in cheesecloth, with a knot at top to use in pulling the cooked fish out of bouillon when it is done. This net keeps fish firmly in shape while cooking. Add dry white wine to simmering bouillon. Lower fish into kettle and cook. Bring again to a simmer and cook 10 minutes per pound of salmon. Remove salmon from pot, and place on a large, hot platter. Using great care, slip off cheesecloth. Serve with Egg Sauce. Serves 10 to 12.

Note: This dish can be nicely accented by parsleyed new potatoes, sprigs of parsley, thyme, mint, or watercress, halves of hard-cooked eggs, and thin lemon slices.

Egg Sauce

Butter 1 tablespoon, melted
Flour 1 tablespoon
Bouillon 2 cups from cooking the fish
Heavy cream 3 tablespoons
Lemon juice of ½
Eggs 4, hard-cooked and chopped
Butter 1 tablespoon
Parsley ½ teaspoon finely minced

In a saucepan, melt 1 tablespoon butter; stir in flour, and cook until bubbly; add bouillon. Stir and cook until thickened and smooth. Add cream and lemon juice, and fold in eggs. Stir in 1 tablespoon butter. Spoon into sauce tureen and sprinkle with finely minced parsley. Serve very hot. Makes about 2 cups.

Salmon Kebobs

Salmon steaks 2½ pounds
Large cucumbers 3
Dry white wine ½ cup
Soy sauce 3 tablespoons
Sugar 1 teaspoon
Butter 2 tablespoons, melted

Cut salmon into 1½-inch chunks; remove bones. Peel and cut cucumbers in half; remove seeds and cut cucumbers into 1-inch chunks. Combine wine, soy sauce, sugar, and butter; pour over salmon and cucumber chunks. Mix and allow to marinate in refrigerator for at least 1 hour. Place on skewers alternately with salmon and cucumber until skewers are filled. Broil about 4 inches above moderately hot coals. Turn skewers and baste with marinade until salmon is lightly browned all over. Serves 5 to 6.

Shrimp and Poached Salmon

Salmon steaks or fillets 2 pounds
Water 1 cup
White wine 1 cup
Thyme pinch
Bay leaf 1
Salt 1 teaspoon
Fish stock 2 cups strained
Butter 2 tablespoons, melted
Flour 2 tablespoons
Egg yolks 2, beaten slightly
Lemon juice 1 tablespoon
Parsley 2 teaspoons minced
Shrimp 1 5-ounce can
Paprika garnish
Lemon cut into slices

Place cleaned salmon in skillet; add water, wine, thyme, bay leaf, and salt. Bring to a boil, turn heat down, cover, and simmer gently for 12 minutes or until steaks are done (they should flake easily when tested with a fork). Strain the fish stock from skillet and set aside. Melt butter in a skillet over low heat; gradually stir in flour until smooth; slowly stir in fish stock; cook gently until thick and creamy, stirring constantly. Mix egg yolks, lemon juice, and parsley together and stir slowly into sauce. Add drained shrimp and cook gently for 3 minutes. Place salmon steaks on a platter and spoon sauce over them. Garnish with paprika and lemon slices. Serves 6.

Kokt Lox (Poached Salmon)

Salmon 1 2-pound cut
Salt to taste
Stock:
    Water 1 quart
    White vinegar 3 tablespoons
    Salt 1 tablespoon
    Peppercorns 5
    Whole allspice 3
    Bay leaf 1
    Onion 1
    Carrot 1
Dill sprigs 10
Tomatoes sliced
Cucumber slices

Clean salmon; sprinkle with salt. Combine all stock ingredients and boil, covered, 15 minutes. Wrap fish and dill in cheesecloth and place in boiling pot; skim. Cover and simmer fish 15 to 20 minutes. Remove carefully and place on platter. Garnish with tomato and cucumber and serve with Hollandaise Sauce. Serves 4 to 6.

Hollandaise Sauce

Egg yolks 4
Hot water 3 tablespoons
Butter ½ cup, melted
Salt to taste
Pepper to taste
Lemon juice 2 tablespoons

Beat egg yolks and water in double boiler over hot water for 1 minute. Melt butter; pour into egg mixture, season with salt and pepper, stirring until thick. Add lemon juice to taste. Serve immediately or, if not served directly, keep uncovered. Makes about 1 cup.

Note: This is a delicious sauce for all kinds of boiled or poached fish.

Salmon Tarragon

Fresh salmon   1, 3 pounds
Stock:
    Water   2 cups
    Tarragon wine vinegar   ½ cup
    Onion   1 tablespoon minced
    Peppercorns   4
    Salt   to taste
    Pepper   to taste
Parsley sprigs   garnish

Clean salmon; wrap in cheesecloth and place on rack in large kettle. Combine next 6 ingredients and pour over fish. Cover and simmer 45 minutes. Lift fish out carefully; remove skin. Serve either hot or well chilled. Decorate platter with parsley. Top salmon with spoonfuls of Tarragon Sauce. Serves 6.

Tarragon Sauce

Sour cream   1 cup
Tarragon wine vinegar   2 tablespoons
Salt   to taste
Pepper   to taste
Scallions   1 tablespoon cut
Sugar   ½ teaspoon

Combine all ingredients and mix thoroughly. Makes 1 cup.

Salmon with Dillweed and Sour Cream

Whole salmon   2 pounds
Stock:
    Water   enough to cover fish
    Seasoning salt   ½ teaspoon
    Celery seed   ½ teaspoon
    Parsley   ½ teaspoon shredded
    Salt   1 teaspoon
    Peppercorns   4

Clean salmon; place on rack in large kettle. Combine rest of ingredients and pour over fish. Cover and simmer in stock for 24 minutes. Carefully remove salmon to platter and serve either hot or cold with Dillweed and Sour Cream Sauce. Serves 4.

Dillweed and Sour Cream Sauce

Sour cream   1 cup
Dillweed   1 teaspoon
Eschalot wine vinegar   1 tablespoon
Salt   ¼ teaspoon

Mix all ingredients well. Serve with hot or cold salmon. Makes 1 cup.

Salmon Hotel Pontchartrain

Pan-sized salmon 1
Salt pinch
Olive oil 2 tablespoons
Stewed tomatoes 2 tablespoons chopped and drained
Oregano pinch
Onion 1 teaspoon chopped fine
Chablis wine 2 tablespoons
Parsley 1 teaspoon finely chopped
Anchovy fillet 1, chopped
Garlic clove 1, crushed
Parsley sprig 1
Lemon cut into wedges

Preheat oven to 400°. Remove scales and fins from salmon's belly and back, leaving head and tail intact; debone, wash, salt the cavity, and set aside. Mix next 7 ingredients and stuff cavity of salmon. Brush 1 side of foil with a little oil and place salmon in the center on its belly side. Add garlic to top of salmon. Wrap the foil around and make a double fold to seal so that juices will not run out when cooking. Arrange package in a pan and bake for 20 minutes. Remove from oven; discard foil and garlic, reserving juice; skin completely. Place salmon on platter. Pour juice from package over it. Garnish with parsley and lemon. Serves 1.

Salmon with Oysters or Clams

Pan-sized salmon   4
Salt   to taste
Pepper   to taste
Oysters or clams   ½ cup
Cracker crumbs   ½ cups finely chopped
Butter   2 tablespoons, melted
Salt   1 teaspoon
Sweet pickles or relish   2 tablespoons chopped
Lemon juice   2 tablespoons
White wine or water   ½ cup
Wine and Butter Sauce   ½ cup

Preheat oven to 350°. Scale and remove back and belly fins from salmon, leaving heads and tails intact; wash and dry salmon then salt and pepper cavities; set aside. Combine rest of ingredients; mix lightly and stuff each cavity. Place fish in an oiled baking pan and bake for 20 to 25 minutes or until flesh flakes easily when tested with a fork. Brush fish with Wine and Butter Sauce while baking. Serves 4.

Wine and Butter Sauce

Butter   6 tablespoons
White wine or vermouth   1 tablespoon
Parsley   2 tablespoons

Melt ingredients together. Makes about ½ cup.

Country-Baked Salmon

Pan-sized salmon 4
Salt to taste
Lemon juice squeeze
Butter 4 tablespoons, melted
Marjoram ¼ teaspoon
Zucchini 1, sliced
Green onion ½ cup chopped
Tomato 1, chopped
Parsley sprigs 2, chopped
Mushrooms ½ cup sliced
Salt to taste
Pepper to taste
Bacon strips 4
Canned tomatoes 2 cups

Preheat oven to 450°. Scale salmon; remove back and belly fins, leaving head and tail intact; wash fish. Rub salt and lemon juice over salmon. Melt butter; mix lightly with next 8 ingredients. Stuff each cavity with mixture, reserving some for sauce; lace closed (to keep the stuffing in). Place salmon in lightly oiled baking pan. Lay a bacon strip on top of each salmon; surround salmon with remaining stuffing mixture and add tomatoes. Bake salmon until meat flakes easily (about 20 minutes). Remove salmon to a hot platter. Serve sauce separately. Serves 4.

Note: Juices can be thickened with cornstarch or flour. Add chopped garlic and a preferred wine to this sauce to make it even richer.

Salmon Puget Sound

Pan-sized salmon 6
Butter or margarine ½ cup
Lemon juice 2 tablespoons
Lemon pepper seasoning to taste
Salt to taste
Orange cut into wedges
Lime cut into wedges
New potatoes cooked and garnished with parsley

Preheat oven to 350°. Scale and remove salmons' back and belly fins, leaving heads and tails intact; wash salmon. Arrange fish in a well-oiled shallow baking pan. Combine butter, lemon juice, and lemon pepper; heat just until melted. Brush inside and outside of each fish with butter mixture and sprinkle with salt. Bake for 25 minutes. When fish flakes easily, remove from oven; arrange fish on a platter and pour remaining butter mixture over fish. Garnish with orange and lime wedges. Serve with potatoes and Brown Butter Sauce. Serves 6.

Brown Butter Sauce

Butter or margarine 2 tablespoons, melted
Onion 1 thin slice
Flour 2 tablespoons
Beef broth 1 cup*
Salt ¼ teaspoon
Pepper ⅛ teaspoon

Heat butter in skillet over low heat until golden brown. Add onion; cook and stir until onion is tender; discard onion. Blend in flour; cook over low heat, stirring until flour is deep brown; remove from heat. Stir in broth; heat to boiling, stirring constantly. Boil and stir 1 minute. Stir in salt and pepper. Makes 1 cup.
*Beef broth can be made by dissolving 1 beef bouillon cube in 1 cup boiling water, or you can use canned beef broth (bouillon).

Salmon Just for Two

Pan-sized salmon 2
Butter melted
Oil
Salt to taste
Pepper to taste
Dillweed to taste
Lemon juice squeeze

Scale salmon and remove back and belly fins leaving heads and tails on. Wash and dry cavities. Brush cavities with butter and oil inside and out; sprinkle salt, pepper, and dill lightly inside; finish with a squeeze of lemon juice. Place salmon on preheated, oiled broiling pan, about 6 inches from heating element. Broil each side 1 minute per ounce; if fish is frozen, double the broiling time. Baste with juices from pan throughout broiling. Place fish on a warm platter and serve. Serves 2.

Minted Pan-Sized Salmon

Pan-sized salmon 4
Butter ¼ cup
Honey 1 tablespoon
Lemon juice 4 tablespoons
Mint leaves 3 tablespoons chopped
Savory ⅛ teaspoon
Salt to taste
Pepper to taste
Mint sprigs garnish
Citrus cut into wedges

Scale and remove back and belly fins, leaving heads and tails intact; wash salmon. Place fish on a well-greased broiling pan. Combine next 7 ingredients and heat until butter has melted; baste fish. Place pan about 4 inches below heat. Broil until golden brown (about 8 to 10 minutes) and baste often while broiling. Serve on a platter decorated with mint and citrus. Serves 4.

Dill Sautéed Salmon

Pan-sized salmon 1
Salt to taste
Pepper to taste
Evaporated milk
Bread crumbs handful
Butter or margarine to taste
Lemon juice from ½ lemon
Dill or parsley chopped, to taste

Scale and remove back and belly fins, leaving head and tail intact; wash salmon. Take cleaned salmon and salt and pepper inside of cavity. Dip fish in milk then dust with bread crumbs. Sauté salmon in a liberal amount of butter. If using butter, maintain a hot temperature just under blackening. Turn when first side has browned. Test with a fork when frying is completed (normally 2 minutes to a side). Remove fish from pan. With juices remaining in pan, add lemon juice and dill; stir quickly over low heat. The sauce is ready to be poured over fish. Serves 1.

Rosellini's Salmon Amandine

Pan-sized salmon 2
Salt 1 teaspoon
Milk 1 cup
Flour handful
Butter 4 tablespoons, melted
Blanched almonds ½ cup
Lemon juice squeeze

Remove back and belly fins, leaving heads and tails intact; wash salmon. Combine salt and milk, and dip salmon in mixture. Roll in flour. Brown on both sides in 2 tablespoons of butter over medium heat, cooking approximately 10 minutes. Transfer salmon onto a warm platter. Melt 2 tablespoons of butter in a skillet. Stir in almonds and cook until golden brown. Spoon almonds over fish, ending with a squeeze of lemon. Serves 2.

Note: Our favorite way to prepare pan-sized salmon!

Sautéed Silvers

Pan-sized salmon 2
Salt to taste
Pepper to taste
Flour dust
Lemon thin slices
Butter 4 tablespoons, melted
Oil 2 tablespoons
Cucumber peeled and diced
Sour cream garnish
Baby beets garnish

Remove back and belly fins, leaving heads and tails intact; wash salmon. Salt and pepper inside cavities. Dust fish lightly with flour and place lemon slices inside cavities. Now fry in mixture of butter and oil over a medium heat at 350° until golden brown. Allow about 1 minute (1½ minutes if frozen) per ounce of salmon on each side; turn and cook until thickest part of meat is no longer transparent and flesh flakes easily. Remove from heat. Serve with cucumber and sour cream mixture and baby beets. Serves 2.

Variation: Place the cooked fish on a bed of freshly cooked spinach. Then sprinkle lemon juice, tarragon, and minced garlic over entire dish.

Salmon Meunière

Pan-sized salmon 4
Salt to taste
Pepper to taste
Butter 4 tablespoons, melted
Rosemary ½ teaspoon
Olive oil 2 tablespoons
Heavy cream
Cracker crumbs 2 cups
Large lemon juice from 1
Sauterne 2 tablespoons
Parsley ⅓ cup chopped

Preheat oven to 350°. Scale and remove salmon's back and belly fins leaving heads and tails on; wash and dry salmon then salt and pepper cavities; set aside. Melt butter in a large skillet; add rosemary and olive oil. Dip fish in cream then roll in crumbs. Sauté fish for about 8 minutes. Place fish in a baking dish. Add lemon juice and sauterne into the skillet and add parsley; stir for 1 minute over medium heat; pour over salmon. Place fish in oven for 5 minutes. Serve fish on a warmed platter. Serves 4.

Coos Bay Salmon Barbecue

Pan-sized salmon 4
Salt to taste
Catsup ½ cup
Water ¼ cup
Lemon juice ¼ cup
Molasses ⅛ cup
Dry mustard ½ teaspoon
Butter ¼ cup
Small onion 1, minced
Soy sauce 1 tablespoon

Scale salmon and remove back and belly fins leaving heads and tails on; wash and salt inside of cavities. Prepare charcoal or pit fire. Oil grill. Mix all remaining ingredients for sauce in pan on fire. Allow sauce to simmer for 10 minutes. When fire is ready, place grill over fire. Oil fish and baste with sauce. Fish should be about 6 to 8 inches from heat; let fish broil about 5 minutes to a side, basting often; fish is cooked when flesh in center is no longer transparent. Just before serving, brush a final coating of sauce over fish. Serves 4.

Jellied Salmon

Stock:
    Celery stalk 1, finely chopped
    Green onions 8, finely chopped
    Garlic clove 1, finely chopped
    Parsley ½ cup chopped
    Salt ½ teaspoon
    Peppercorns 3
    Bay leaf 1
    Thyme ¼ teaspoon
    Marjoram 1 teaspoon
    White wine 1½ cups
    Water 1 quart

Pan-sized salmon 4
Egg white 1, beaten
Unflavored gelatin 1½ teaspoons
Water ½ cup
Fresh asparagus spears
Cucumber 1, unpared and sliced
Radish flowerettes garnish
Lemon juice 2 teaspoons
Mayonnaise 2 cups

Combine first 11 ingredients in a saucepan; bring to boil and then simmer about 20 minutes. Strain broth through a fine sieve and into a flat pan suitable to hold 4 pan-sized salmon. Scale and remove salmon's back and belly fins, leaving heads and tails intact. Place washed fish in flat pan with broth; bring to boil. Reduce heat and poach for 5 to 6 minutes or until fish flake easily with a fork. Remove fish from pan, reserving broth, and place on a platter and chill.

To prepare jelly, reduce broth to 3 cups; clarify with lightly beaten egg white. Strain broth through a fine sieve or cheesecloth. Soften gelatin in water; add to broth. Chill until thick and syrupy. Leaving chilled fish on platter, spoon jelly over plain or decorated fish. Cover fish completely and refrigerate; chill until firm (about 4 hours). To garnish, chop extra jelly and garnish along with asparagus spears cut in 3-inch lengths, cucumber slices, and radish flowerettes. Mix the lemon and mayonnaise and serve in a separate dish. Serves 4.

Poached Pan-Sized Salmon #1

Pan-sized salmon 2
Milk heated, enough to cover fish
Tomato juice splash
Flour 1½ tablespoons
Cold milk ¼ cup
Heavy cream ½ cup
Egg yolks 2, beaten
Butter 1 tablespoon

Scale and remove salmon's back and belly fins; leave heads and tails intact. Clean salmon and place in skillet. Barely cover with hot milk and a splash of tomato juice. Cover and simmer just under boiling point, for about 10 minutes or until fish flakes when tested with a fork. Using slotted spatula, remove to a warm platter. Blend flour and cold milk and add slowly to remaining liquid in skillet. Bring to a simmer, stirring in cream, and heat again to a bubble; make sure that sauce does not stick. Remove from heat and slowly add egg yolks and butter. Stir until blended. Ladle sauce over salmon. Serves 2.

Poached Pan-Sized Salmon #2

Pan-sized salmon 1
Salt to taste
Pepper to taste
Water enough to cover salmon
Peppercorns 3
Bay leaf 1
Onion ½, chopped
Clove 1
Carrot 1, sliced
Lemon cut into slices

Scale and remove salmon's back and belly fins; leave head and tail intact. Wash and dry salmon then salt and pepper cavity. Heat enough water to cover salmon in a small roasting pan; add rest of ingredients except lemon and bring to a boil for 5 minutes. Wrap salmon in cheesecloth, leaving ends long enough to lift fish easily from pan.* Place salmon in boiling water mixture and keep temperature just under boiling point throughout poaching. Allow 1½ minutes per ounce of salmon or 10 to 15 minutes for a 10-ounce salmon. Place fish on a hot platter with lemon slices. Serve with Easy Hollandaise Sauce. Serves 1.

*If you are using a fish poacher pot, you do not need to use cheesecloth method.

Easy Hollandaise Sauce

Butter or margarine   ½ cup
Salt   ¼ teaspoon
Cayenne   dash
Lemon juice   1 tablespoon
Egg yolks   2

Beat butter in top of double boiler (not over heat or hot water) until creamy. Add salt and cayenne. Add lemon juice, a few drops at a time, beating constantly. Add egg yolks, 1 at a time, beating until sauce is light and fluffy. Place over hot, not boiling, water for a few minutes, and stir constantly until glossy.* Serve warm. Makes ¾ cup.

*The water should not touch the top of the pan. Do not let sauce stay over hot water too long.

Poached Salmon with Caviar Sauce

Pan-sized salmon   2
Water   enough to cover fish
Green onions   ½ cup sliced
Celery   1 cup chopped
Clove   1
Bay leaf   1
Salt   to taste
Pepper   to taste

Scale and remove salmon's back and belly fins, leaving heads and tails intact; wash salmon. In a roasting pan or skillet, heat enough water to cover fish; add rest of ingredients and bring to a boil for 5 minutes. Wrap salmon in cheesecloth and place on rack in boiling water mixture; cover and simmer just under boiling point for 10 minutes and no more. Remove fish, reserving broth. Place fish on a hot platter and serve with Caviar Sauce. Serves 2.

Caviar Sauce

Butter   2 tablespoons, melted
Flour   1½ tablespoons
White wine and salmon liquid   ½ cup
Whipping cream   2 tablespoons
Egg yolk   1, slightly beaten
Black caviar   2 tablespoons
Salt   to taste
Pepper   to taste

Melt butter in a small saucepan; add flour to form a roux. Add wine and enough strained liquid from salmon to make a smooth sauce; simmer for 5 to 10 minutes. Remove sauce from heat; add cream and egg yolk. Do not boil. Add caviar, salt, and pepper to sauce and serve separately. Makes about 1 cup.

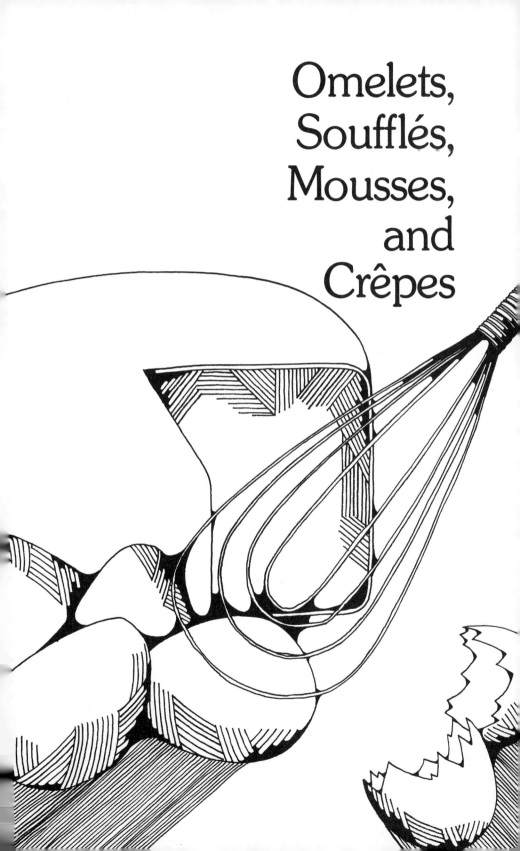

Omelets,
Soufflés,
Mousses,
and
Crêpes

Fluffy Fisherman's Omelet

Salmon 1 7¾-ounce can
Eggs 6, separated
Salmon liquid and water ⅓ cup combined
Parsley 1 tablespoon chopped
Chives 1 teaspoon chopped
Salt ½ teaspoon
Oregano dash
Pepper dash
Butter 2 tablespoons, melted

Preheat oven to 350°. Drain and remove skin and bones from salmon, reserving liquid; flake salmon. Beat egg whites until stiff; set aside. Beat egg yolks until thick and lemon colored; add next 6 ingredients. Add salmon and mix well. Fold into egg white mixture. Pour omelet mixture into hot, buttered 10-inch fry pan and spread evenly. Cook over low heat for 3 to 5 minutes or until lightly browned on bottom. Bake for 2 to 5 minutes or until a knife inserted in the center comes out clean. Cut part way through center of omelet and fold in half. Serve immediately on a warm platter. Serves 6.

Lox and Eggs

Large spanish onion 1, chopped
Green pepper 1, chopped
Mushrooms 2 cups sliced
Butter ½ cup
Smoked salmon (lox) ½ pound, diced
Eggs 8
Heavy cream ¼ cup
Parsley 1 tablespoon chopped
Basil ¼ teaspoon
Tabasco sauce dash
Monosodium glutamate 1 teaspoon
Salt to taste
Pepper ½ teaspoon

Place onion, green pepper, and mushrooms in a heavy skillet; cover skillet and allow vegetables to steam in their own juices, without butter, until they almost stick to pan. Add butter and stir. Add salmon and continue to cook for 1 minute, stirring until salmon becomes light pink. Beat eggs, adding cream, parsley, basil, tabasco, and monosodium glutamate; add egg mixture to skillet. Continue to cook over low heat, stirring constantly, until eggs begin to set but are still creamy. Stir in a little salt and pepper. Serve immediately. Serves 4 to 6.

Simple Salmon Soufflé

Salmon   2 cups cooked and flaked, or 1 15½-ounce can
Butter   3 tablespoons, melted
Flour   3 tablespoons
Evaporated milk   1 cup
Salt   ¼ teaspoon
Eggs   4, separated

Preheat oven to 350°. If using canned salmon, drain, remove skin and bones, and flake. Melt butter in a saucepan over low heat; gradually add flour and milk until thickened. Add salt. Remove from heat and stir in slightly beaten egg yolks; cook gently for another minute; remove from heat. Stir in flaked salmon. Fold in stiffly beaten egg whites, by pouring the cooked mixture into egg whites. Pour into a buttered 2-quart baking dish and bake for 45 to 50 minutes. Serves 6.

The Captain's Curry Soufflé

Salmon   1 15½-ounce can
Butter   2 tablespoons, melted
Flour   3 tablespoons
Milk   1 cup
Thyme   ¼ teaspoon
Curry powder   ½ teaspoon
Salt   to taste
Pepper   to taste
Eggs   4, separated

Preheat oven to 375°. Drain, and remove skin and bones from salmon. In saucepan melt butter, blend in flour, and add milk and seasonings; cook for 2 or 3 minutes; remove from heat. Add yolks and salmon to mixture and stir well. Fold in stiffly beaten egg whites. Put in buttered 1½-quart casserole dish and bake for 35 minutes. Serves 4.

Stirring Salmon Soufflé

Salmon 1 15½-ounce can
Salmon liquid and milk 1 cup
Butter 3 tablespoons, melted
Flour 3 tablespoons
Salt 1 teaspoon
Pepper dash
Nutmeg dash
Eggs 3, separated

Preheat oven to 350°. Drain and flake salmon, saving liquid; remove skin and bones. Melt butter and blend in flour and seasonings. Add liquid gradually and cook until thick and smooth, stirring constantly. Stir a little of the hot sauce into beaten egg yolk and add to sauce, stirring constantly. Add salmon. Beat egg white until stiff but not dry. Fold gently into salmon mixture. Pour into well-greased 1-quart casserole dish and bake for 45 minutes. Serve immediately. Serves 6.

Cottage Salmon Mousse

Salmon 1 15½-ounce can
Unflavored gelatin 1 envelope
Cold water ¼ cup
Water ½ cup, boiling
Mayonnaise ½ cup
Lemon juice 1 tablespoon
Onion 1 tablespoon grated
Tabasco sauce ½ teaspoon
Paprika ¼ teaspoon
Salt 1 teaspoon
Capers 1 tablespoon chopped
Whipping cream ½ cup
Cottage cheese 3 cups
Watercress garnish
Lemon cut into slices
Salmon roe garnish
Dillweed and Sour Cream Sauce (see Index)

Drain, remove skin and bones, and finely chop salmon. Soften gelatin in cold water, add boiling water, and stir until dissolved; let cool. Add mayonnaise, lemon juice, onion, tabasco, paprika, and salt; mix well; chill to consistency of unbeaten egg white. Add salmon and capers and beat well. Whip the cream, fold in salmon mixture, and turn into a 2-quart oiled fish mold. Add cheese to top of mold. Chill until set. Unmold on a serving platter and garnish with watercress, lemon, and salmon roe. Serve with Dillweed and Sour Cream Sauce. Serves 4 to 6.

Salmon Velvet Mousse

Salmon 1 15½-ounce can
Egg whites 4, beaten
Sour cream 1 cup
Salt ¾ teaspoon
Pepper ⅛ teaspoon
Mace ⅛ teaspoon
Chives 2 tablespoons chopped

Preheat oven to 350°. Drain salmon, remove skin and bones, and flake with fork until fine, then rub through coarse sieve. Beat egg whites only until bubbly but not stiff. Place salmon in chilled mixing bowl that is standing in pan of ice water. Gradually add egg whites, stirring gently; gradually add sour cream; continue stirring until texture is smooth; add salt, pepper, and mace. Pour mixture into 5-cup buttered mold; place in pan of hot water; bake for 15 minutes or until set. Unmold on warm platter. Sprinkle chives over mold before serving. Serves 6.

Cold Artichoke Bottoms with Salmon Mousse

Artichoke Bottoms

Large or medium artichokes 6 or 12
Lemon ½
Flour 2 tablespoons
Lemon juice 2 tablespoons
Cold water 4 cups
Salt to taste
Vinaigrette Dressing (see Index)
Paprika sprinkle
Capers garnish
Dill sprigs garnish
Black olives garnish
Black bread buttered

Cut stems of artichokes as close to base as possible; remove first few layers of outer leaves; rub cut parts with ½ lemon. In a large enamel saucepan combine flour, lemon juice, and water. Bring mixture to a boil, add a pinch of salt and artichoke bottoms. Cook for 20 to 30 minutes or until tender. Cool and dry on paper towels. As soon as they are cool enough to handle, remove each choke with a grapefruit spoon and trim artichoke bottoms with a sharp knife. Pour Vinaigrette Dressing over artichoke bottoms. Cover bowl and let bottoms marinate for 2 hours. Drain artichoke bottoms and dry on toweling. Top each artichoke with a dome of Salmon Mousse. Sprinkle lightly with paprika. Make a circle of capers on each dome and top with 2 tiny sprigs of dill and an olive. Chill again and serve cold with buttered black bread. Serves 6.

Salmon Mousse

Salmon   2 cups cooked
Mayonnaise   3 tablespoons
Salt   to taste
Pepper   to taste
Cayenne   dash
Lemon juice   2 teaspoons
Fresh dill   1 tablespoon finely minced

Purée salmon in a blender or put it through the fine blade of a meat grinder. Add rest of ingredients; mix well. Chill mixture for 1 hour; mixture should be quite thick.

Mousse Copenhagen

Fine bread crumbs   3 tablespoons
Eggs   2
Salt   to taste
White pepper   dash
Milk   ¼ cup
Fresh salmon fillets   1 pound
Heavy cream   ¾ cup
Lemon juice   3 tablespoons

Preheat oven to 300°. All ingredients should be at room temperature. Generously butter a 1-quart ring mold, sprinkle with bread crumbs, and shake out excess. Beat egg with salt and pepper; add milk. Remove skin and bones from salmon. Chop and blend in blender together with egg mixture. Add cream to egg mixture, beating slowly with a wooden spoon; add lemon juice. Mixture should be smooth but not liquid. Drop a teaspoonful of mixture into boiling water and cook briefly; if too liquid, thicken with flour; if too thick, thin with milk. Pour into ring mold, cover with foil, and place in pan of hot water, 1 inch deep. Bake for 1 to 1½ hours or until set. Serves 4 to 6.

Note: Hollandaise sauce makes a nice addition to this dish.

Crêpes New Orleans

Salmon 1 15½-ounce can
Onion 1 teaspoon chopped
Butter 3 tablespoons, melted
Flour ¼ cup
Salt ¼ teaspoon
White pepper dash
Nutmeg dash
Salmon liquid and milk 1½ cups combined
Egg yolks 2, beaten
Parmesan cheese 2 tablespoons grated
Sherry 2 tablespoons
Crêpes 12
Lemon 2 slices each cut into sixths
Parsley garnish

Preheat oven to 350°. Drain, remove skin and bones, reserve liquid, and flake salmon. Cook onion in butter until tender. Blend in flour and seasonings. Add salmon liquid and milk mixture gradually and cook until thick, stirring constantly. Stir a little of the hot sauce into the egg yolks; add to remaining sauce, stirring constantly. Add cheese and sherry and stir until blended. Mix ½ cup of sauce with salmon; blend well. Reserve remaining sauce to serve with crêpes. Prepare crêpes. Spread about 2 tablespoons of salmon mixture on each crêpe; roll like a jelly roll. Place crêpes on a greased 15 x 12-inch cooking sheet. Heat in oven for 10 to 15 minutes. Heat sauce. Arrange crêpes in a circle in a chafing dish. Garnish each crêpe with lemon and parsley. Place sauce in the center and on top of each crêpe. Serves 6.

Crêpes

Flour ¾ cup
Salt ¼ teaspoon
Eggs 2, beaten
Milk 1 cup

Sift dry ingredients together. Combine eggs and milk. Add gradually to flour mixture; stir only until batter is smooth. Drop 2 tablespoons of batter onto a hot and lightly greased griddle or frying pan. Fry about 2 minutes or until crêpe is browned on the underside; turn and fry until bottom is browned. Makes 12.

Salmon Pancakes

Pancake mix 1 cup
Egg 1
Milk 1 cup
Salad oil 1 tablespoon
Salmon 1 7¾-ounce can
White Sauce (see Index)

Combine all ingredients except salmon and sauce. Drain and remove skin and bones from salmon. Stir batter until smooth; add ½ of salmon. Heat pancake griddle, oil lightly, and fry each cake until golden brown on both sides. Add remaining salmon to the prepared white sauce and serve over hot pancakes. Makes about 8 medium cakes. Serves 4.

Note: Sour cream mixed with the remaining salmon also makes a nice sauce for this dish.

Casseroles
and
Stuffings

Salmon Ring with Dill Sauce and Peas

Water 4 cups
Salt 1 tablespoon
Pepper ¼ teaspoon
Parsley sprigs 3
Medium onion 1, sliced
Bay leaf 1
Celery stalks 2, chopped
White wine ¼ cup or
     Lemon 2 slices
Fresh salmon 2 pounds
Green peas 2 cups cooked
White Sauce

Pour water into large kettle; add next 7 ingredients. Bring to a boil for 5 minutes. Lower heat and place cleaned salmon in wire basket or poacher in kettle, and let simmer until tender (about 30 minutes). Do not let stock come to full boil. Remove fish from kettle; cool and remove skin and bones; flake fine; reserve stock. Cook peas. Now prepare White Sauce; add salmon to it and mix well. Pour into a greased 5-cup ring mold. Set into a pan of hot water; bake at 325° for 45 minutes or until set. Fill center of fish ring with peas and serve with Dill Sauce. Serves 6.

White Sauce

Butter 2 tablespoons
Flour 2 tablespoons
Milk 1 cup
Salt to taste
Pepper to taste
Eggs 3, beaten

Melt butter and blend in flour. Add milk and cook, stirring 4 minutes or until thickened; add salt and pepper to taste. Blend in beaten eggs.

Dill Sauce

Fish stock ½ cup strained
Butter 2 tablespoons
Flour 2 tablespoons
Milk ¾ cup
Fresh dill 3 teaspoons chopped or
    Dried dill 1 teaspoon
Lemon juice ½ teaspoon
Salt to taste
Pepper to taste

Cook first 4 ingredients as for White Sauce, stirring until thickened. Add remaining ingredients. Makes about 1 cup.

Toasted Salmon Loaves

Salmon 2 cups cooked
Dry bread crumbs 1 cup
Cheddar cheese 1 cup grated
Eggs 2, beaten
Milk ⅔ cup
Butter 2 tablespoons, melted
Onion 2 tablespoons chopped
Seasoning salt ½ teaspoon
Parsley ½ teaspoon
Butter 2 tablespoons, melted
Stuffed olives sliced
Cream of mushroom soup 1 10½-ounce can
Milk

Flake salmon; add next 8 ingredients; mix well and shape mixture into 6 loaves. Melt 2 tablespoons of butter in heavy skillet. Over medium heat, sauté salmon loaves, turning on all sides until golden brown and cooked through. Decorate loaves with olives. Dilute a can of mushroom soup with a little milk and heat; pour over loaves. Serves 6.

Salmon Loaf with Shrimp Sauce

Salmon 2 cups cooked
Lemon juice 1 tablespoon
Butter 2 tablespoons, melted
Flour 2 tablespoons
Milk 1½ cups
Salt ½ teaspoon
Eggs, 2, beaten
Parsley 2 tablespoons minced
Rolled oats 1 cup
Frozen shrimp soup 1 10½-ounce can

Preheat oven to 350°. Flake salmon; sprinkle with lemon juice. Melt butter in saucepan, blend in flour, and stir until thick and smooth. Add milk stirring constantly. Stir in salmon, salt, eggs, parsley, and rolled oats. Pour mixture into well-greased 9-inch loaf pan. Bake for 30 minutes. Heat soup in double boiler and pour over loaf. Serves 4 to 6.

Salmonburgers

Salmon 1 15½-ounce can
Salmon liquid ⅓ cup
Onion ½ cup chopped
Fat or oil ¼ cup, melted
Dry bread crumbs ⅓ cup
Eggs 2, beaten
Parsley ¼ cup chopped
Powdered mustard 1 teaspoon
Salt ½ teaspoon
Dry bread crumbs ½ cup
Mayonnaise or salad dressing ⅓ cup
Sweet pickle 1 tablespoon chopped
Hamburger rolls 6, buttered

Drain salmon, reserving liquid; flake and remove skin and bones. Cook onion in fat until tender. Add salmon liquid, crumbs, eggs, parsley, mustard, salt, and salmon; mix well. Shape into 6 burgers. Roll in crumbs. Fry in hot fat in a heavy fry pan about 4 inches from hot coals for 3 minutes. Turn carefully and fry 3 to 4 minutes longer or until brown. Drain on absorbent paper. Combine mayonnaise and pickle. Place burgers on bottom ½ of each roll. Top with approximately 1 tablespoon mayonnaise mixture; top with other ½ of roll. Serves 6.

Salmon à la King

Salmon 1 15½-ounce can
Butter ½ cup, melted
Celery ½ cup chopped
Green pepper ½ cup chopped
Flour ¼ cup
Salt ½ teaspoon
Salmon liquid and milk 1½ cups combined
Mushrooms 1 cup cooked and sliced
Pimiento 2 tablespoons chopped
Patty shell, toast, or cooked rice

Drain salmon, reserving liquid; remove skin and bones and break into small chunks. Melt butter in a pan; add celery and green pepper; cook over low heat until vegetables are tender. Gradually add flour and salt; stir until smooth. Slowly add salmon liquid and milk; cook gently, stirring until sauce is thick and smooth. Add salmon, mushrooms, and pimiento. Heat mixture and serve in a patty shell. Serves 6.

Salmon Noodles Yukon

Salmon 1 15½-ounce can
Medium-sized noodles 1 8-ounce package
Butter or margarine 2 tablespoons, melted
Flour 2 tablespoons
Milk 1 cup
Tabasco dash
Salt to taste
Pepper to taste
Fresh bread crumbs 1 cup
Butter or margarine ¼ cup, melted

Preheat oven to 350°. Drain and flake salmon; remove skin and bones. Cook noodles according to package directions; drain well and rinse. Grease a 2-quart casserole. In saucepan melt 2 tablespoons of butter; stir in flour. Gradually stir in milk and cook, stirring until sauce is smooth and thickened. Stir in salmon, tabasco, salt, and pepper. Arrange alternate layers of salmon, sauce, and noodles in casserole, finishing with sauce. In a small bowl mix crumbs with butter; sprinkle over mixture in casserole. Bake for 30 minutes. Serves 6.

Salmon Anne

Salmon 1 15½-ounce can
Salmon liquid
Thin spaghetti 1 8-ounce package
Butter or margarine 4 tablespoons, melted
Mushrooms ½ pound sliced
Flour 4 tablespoons
Salt ¾ teaspoon
Pepper ⅛ teaspoon
Curry powder ¼ teaspoon
Milk 4 cups
Salt to taste
Lemon juice of ½
Sherry 2 tablespoons
Cheese 4 tablespoons shredded
Fresh bread crumbs ½ cup
Parsley garnish

Preheat oven to 350°. Drain salmon, reserving liquid; flake and remove skin and bones. Cook spaghetti in large quantity of rapidly boiling water for 10 minutes, or until barely tender. Drain and rinse well with cold water; empty into 2-quart casserole. In a large skillet melt butter and sauté mushrooms for 5 minutes. Stir in flour, salt, pepper, and curry powder. Gradually stir in milk and cook, stirring, until sauce is smooth and slightly thickened. Stir in salmon liquid; add salmon. Add salt to taste and stir in lemon juice and sherry. Pour most of the sauce from the skillet into the casserole and toss with spaghetti. Make a hole in center of spaghetti and empty remaining salmon and mushrooms into hole. Combine cheese and bread crumbs and sprinkle over top. Bake for 30 minutes. Garnish with parsley before serving. Serves 6.

Salmon Archiduc

Salmon 2 cups cooked and flaked or 1 15½-ounce can
Onion ¼ cup minced
Butter ¼ cup, melted
Flour 2 tablespoons
Salmon liquid and milk 4½ cups combined*
Salt ½ teaspoon
Freshly ground black pepper ¼ teaspoon
Cayenne dash
Heavy cream ½ cup
Sherry ¼ cup
Cognac 2 tablespoons
Parsley 1 tablespoon finely chopped
Toast points or rice

If using canned salmon, drain, remove skin and bones, and reserve liquid; flake. In a saucepan sauté onion in butter until transparent. Stir in flour; remove from heat. Bring milk and salmon liquid to boil and add to onion mixture. Return to heat stirring constantly until sauce is thick and smooth. Stir in next 6 ingredients. Fold in salmon and parsley and heat until very hot. Serve on toast points. Serves 4.

*If using fresh cooked salmon, use 4½ cups milk.

Curry 'n' Salmon

Salmon   1 15½-ounce can
Onion   ¼ cup chopped
Butter   3 tablespoons, melted
Flour   3 tablespoons
Curry powder   1½ teaspoons
Salt   ½ teaspoon
Ginger   ¼ teaspoon
Pepper   dash
Salmon liquid and milk   2 cups combined
Rice   3 cups cooked

Drain salmon, remove skin and bones, and reserve liquid; break into large chunks. Cook onion in butter until tender. Blend in flour and seasonings. Add salmon liquid and milk gradually and cook until thick, stirring constantly. Add salmon; blend and heat. Serve over rice. Serves 6.

Note: There are many excellent condiments for accompanying curry. Among them: chopped hard-cooked eggs, shredded toasted coconut, chopped nuts, chopped green pepper, chopped tomatoes, fried noodles, chopped onions, crystalized ginger, sieved hard-cooked egg yolks.

Salmon Newburg

Salmon 1½ cups cooked
Butter 4 tablespoons, melted
Flour 4 tablespoons
Milk 2 cups
Egg yolks 2, slightly beaten
Salt ½ teaspoon
Pepper ⅛ teaspoon
Sherry ¼ cup
Tabasco sauce dash
Rice, noodles, or toast

Flake salmon in rather large pieces. Melt butter in a pan and blend in flour; do not brown. Slowly add milk, stirring constantly; cook over medium heat until slightly thickened and smooth; add fish. Remove from heat and slowly add egg yolks. Return to heat and cook 3 minutes longer. Add salt and pepper. Before serving add sherry and tabasco. Serve over rice. Serves 4 to 6.

Creamed Salmon au Gratin

Salmon   2 cups cooked and flaked or 1 15½-ounce can
Onions   ¼ cup finely minced
Butter   3 tablespoons, melted
Flour   3 tablespoons
Milk   1 cup, boiling
Dry white wine or dry white vermouth   ¼ cup
Salmon liquid   canned (optional)
Salt   ¼ teaspoon
Pepper   pinch
Oregano   ¼ teaspoon
Whipping cream   5 tablespoons
Mushrooms   6 sliced and sautéed
Eggs   2 hard-cooked and sliced
Swiss cheese   ¼ cup grated
Butter   1 tablespoon

Preheat oven to 425°. If using canned salmon, drain, reserve the liquid, flake, and remove skin and bones. Sauté onions in butter in saucepan over low heat for 5 minutes, until tender. Stir in flour and cook slowly for 2 minutes. Remove from heat. Beat in boiling milk, then add wine, salmon liquid, and seasonings. Bring sauce to boil over moderately high heat, stirring constantly. Boil for 3 minutes until alcohol evaporates and sauce has thickened. Thin with cream, 1 tablespoon at a time, until sauce is desired consistency; season to taste. Fold salmon, mushrooms, and eggs into sauce. Pour into a greased 3-quart baking dish. Sprinkle with cheese and dot with butter. Bake in upper part of oven for 15 minutes, or until top is golden brown. Serves 4 to 6.

Shrimp and Salmon Newburg

Fresh salmon   2 cups cooked*
Butter   4 tablespoons, melted
Flour   4 tablespoons
Light cream   3 cups
Salt   dash
Pepper   dash
Dry mustard   1 teaspoon
Paprika   1 teaspoon
Tarragon   ½ teaspoon
Egg yolks   4
Sherry   2 tablespoons
Cognac   1 tablespoon
Parmesan cheese   ¼ cup grated
Shrimp   2 cups cooked
Rice   cooked

Break salmon into large pieces. Melt butter, stir in flour, and cook without browning for 3 minutes. Add cream and stir over low heat until mixture comes to a boil. Add seasonings; simmer for 6 minutes, stirring occasionally. Beat egg yolks in a bowl and gradually add hot mixture to yolks, beating constantly. Return to saucepan and add sherry, cognac, salmon, cheese, and shrimp. Heat and stir gently until all is hot. Be sure to use a low heat so the eggs do not curdle. Serve on rice. Serves 4 to 6.
*Do not use canned salmon.

Deep Dish Salmon Pie

Salmon   2 cups cooked or 1 15½-ounce can
Green pea soup   2 10½-ounce cans
Salmon liquid and milk   ⅔ cup combined*
Small potatoes   1 16-ounce can, drained
Small onions   1 8-ounce can
Parsley   ½ teaspoon
Pepper   ⅛ teaspoon
Celery salt   ¼ teaspoon
Refrigerator biscuits   1 7½-ounce package

Preheat oven to 400°. If using canned salmon, drain, remove skin and bones, and reserve liquid. In a saucepan, mix soup and salmon liquid and milk mixture. Stir until smooth; add salmon, potatoes, onions, and seasonings. Heat until mixture begins to simmer, stirring frequently. Pour into a 2-quart casserole. Top with biscuits. Bake for 15 to 20 minutes, or until biscuits are golden brown. Serves 4.
*If using fresh cooked salmon, use ⅔ cup milk.

Zesty Mushroom Stuffing

Onion ¼ cup minced
Celery ¼ cup, minced
Butter ¼ cup, melted
Fresh mushrooms ½ pound, sliced
Parsley 1 tablespoon minced
Crackers 2 cups coarsely crushed
Poultry seasoning ¼ teaspoon
Dillweed ¼ teaspoon
Salt ¼ teaspoon

In a large skillet sauté onion and celery in butter until golden. Add mushrooms and cook for 3 minutes. Add remaining ingredients; mix well. Enough for 4- to 6-pound fish.

Oyster or Clam Stuffing

Oysters or clams ½ cup chopped
Fine cracker crumbs 2 cups
Butter 2 tablespoons, melted
Salt 1 teaspoon
Pickle 2 teaspoons chopped
Onion 1 tablespoon minced
Lemon juice 2 tablespoons
Water ½ cup

Drain oysters or clams, if canned, reserving liquid. Mix all ingredients in order given. If dressing seems dry add more water. The oyster or clam liquid can be used as part of liquid ingredients. Enough for 3- to 4-pound fish.

Savory Stuffing

Celery   ¾ cup chopped
Onion   3 tablespoons chopped
Butter   6 tablespoons, melted
Bread crumbs   4 cups
Salt   1 teaspoon
Pepper   ⅛ teaspoon
Savory   1 teaspoon
Parsley   1 teaspoon
Milk, water, or fish stock   2 tablespoons

Cook celery and onion in butter for about 5 minutes or until tender. Mix with all other ingredients. Enough for 6-pound fish.

Down Home Stuffing

Bread crumbs   1 cup
Hot water   ½ cup
Butter   ¼ cup, melted
Salt   ¼ teaspoon
Onion   ¼, minced
Sage   ¼ teaspoon
Pepper   ⅛ teaspoon

Mix all ingredients together. This recipe is suitable for stuffing small fish or for spooning small amounts on fillets or steaks. If you are preparing a steak, bake at 450° for 10 minutes per inch of thickness. Enough for a 2-pound fish, fillet, or steak.

Raisin' Heck Stuffing

Butter 3 tablespoons, melted
Bread crumbs 3 cups soft
Water 2 cups, boiling
Raisins ½ cup
Walnuts ½ cup chopped
Egg 1, beaten
Salt 1 teaspoon
Pepper ⅛ teaspoon
Marjoram ½ teaspoon

Pour butter over crumbs and mix lightly. Pour boiling water over raisins and allow to stand for 5 minutes. Drain raisins and mix with nuts, egg, salt, pepper, and marjoram. Mix with crumbs. Enough for 3- to 4-pound fish.

Irish Green Stuffing

Frozen chopped spinach 1 12-ounce package
Small onion 1, minced
Butter 1 tablespoon
Salt to taste
Egg 1, beaten
Day-old bread crumbs ½ cup

Cook frozen spinach as directed on package, adding onion and cooking until tender. Drain. Add butter and salt; cool. Add beaten egg and enough of the crumbs to hold mixture together. Enough for a 3-pound fish.

Sour Cream Stuffing

Chopped celery ¾ cup
Chopped onion ½ cup
Melted fat or oil ¼ cup
Bread crumbs 4 cups, toasted*
Sour cream ½ cup
Peeled lemon ¼ cup diced
Lemon rind 2 tablespoons grated
Salt 1 teaspoon
Paprika 1 teaspoon

Cook celery and onion in fat until tender. Combine all ingredients and mix thoroughly. Makes approximately 1 quart of stuffing. Enough for a 3- to 4-pound fish.
*Commercial herb-seasoned croutons may be substituted for bread crumbs.

Wine –
Companion
to Seafood

Wine—Companion to Seafood

by Tom Stockley

There is little doubt that wine belongs on the dinner table with seafood. The Europeans have been happily aware of this fact for centuries. A Frenchman, for example, faced with a platter of oysters on the half shell for a first course, would naturally reach for a chilled bottle of the dry and tart Muscadet. Or, perhaps his choice would be the crisp and full Chablis, universally accepted as the wine to accompany shellfish.

The Italian, served up an order of big tender scampi in a seaside restaurant, would call to the waiter for his finest bottle of Soave, that charming and dry wine from Verona.

An Alsatian confronted with one of his regional favorites, pike poached in Riesling, would expect one of the great Alsatian whites to be glittering in the glass next to his plate.

In other countries as well, seafoods inevitably call for wine, not only on the table, but frequently in the preparation. America, being a newer country, has naturally been slower to pair up cuisine with the juice of the grape. But the wine revolution in recent years has sent Americans on a "crash course" of wine appreciation to the point where wine lists in restaurants are the rule, not the exception, and housewives doing the weekly shopping pick up a bottle of wine as naturally as a quart of milk.

Despite a late start in the discovery of wine, Americans have one important advantage over their European counterparts: the fantastic availability of wines on local shelves. Where a resident of a Rhine River town in Germany may only have his local wines to choose from, the average United States resident can drive to the local wine shop and have the entire world of wine making at his fingertips. It all makes for an exciting and international adventure and one that should be explored by anyone interested in great dining.

The big decision, of course, is which wine to serve with which seafood dish. Our blessing of abundant wines at the shop can become confusing simply because there are so many from which to choose. But it need not be a perplexing problem, even for the person with little knowledge of wine. It is merely a matter of enjoying what you like best and not being intimidated by traditions and rules established years ago.

In truth, almost any white dinner wine can be served with seafood without insulting anyone's taste buds. Nor do you have to restrict yourself to whites. Many rosé wines, particularly the drier ones, are fine with seafood. The exception to all this brings us to the one and only rule to be found in this chapter: *Never drink red wines with fish!* We are not inflicting ancient wine snobbery on you. It is a simple and plain fact that the oiliness of most fish seems to react chemically with red wine. It produces a somewhat bitter and unpleasant taste. There are exceptions, of course, but why subject yourself to an unhappy combination? Stick to the whites and some rosés.

And, to get you started in the right direction, we will group the white wines into three categories and include suggestions on which dishes go best with each. As this book is primarily devoted to that noble and delicious creature from the sea, the salmon, we will gear our remarks toward recipes using that favorite of seafood lovers. However, the same comments on pairing up wine with salmon would apply to most seafood.

One final remark: If there seems to be an overemphasis on California wines, it should be noted that the author has no ulterior motive for promoting products from that particular state. It is just that California is responsible for approximately seventy percent of the wine sold in the United States. Further, it is readily available, offers a wide variety of wine styles, and frequently presents the best price.

Light Whites

It should not be insulting to call these our "everyday wines." They are, indeed, the type of wines you can afford on a regular basis and, because of their relatively unsophisticated character, are just the ticket for most seafood meals. Refreshing and easy to enjoy, these light wines come into their own with the less elaborate salmon recipes such as the broiled and sautéed versions. A poached salmon, revealing salmon in perhaps its most subdued role, would be overwhelmed by some heavier wines. But any of the following would do the salmon on your plate great honor.

Chablis: Not to be confused with the costly classic Chablis of France, this designation on a bottle from California usually means a soft, slightly dry white wine produced from a blend of three or more grapes. It appears in inexpensive jugs and corked fifths and is sometimes labeled Mountain White. Los Hermanos Chablis is a winner in the jug category while several, including Souverain, Beaulieu, and Christian Brothers, bring it to a higher level in fifths.

Sauterne: This is another confusing name as it is nothing like the French Sauternes at all. It would be difficult to tell it apart from Chablis in a blind tasting as it is also a blended wine in California.

Grey Riesling: This Riesling is one of the most popular seafood wines at San Francisco's Fisherman's Wharf and other seaside restaurants. It is not really a Riesling but, rather, a soft and mildly flavored wine ideally suited for salmon and shellfish. Wente Brothers seems to have the market cornered although other vintners do well by it, too.

Sylvaner: Often overshadowed by its more famous cousin, the Johannisberg Riesling, Sylvaner is actually the main Rhine-type grape grown in California. It also is responsible for excellent wines in Alsace, France, as well as Germany. It is a fragrant, fresh white with a delicate flavor. It is apt to be labeled merely as Riesling, Sylvaner, Franken Riesling, or under its true name.

French Colombard: Frequently used in blending whites such as California Chablis, this wine has recently come into its own and is often seen under its own name. It is a light, dry, and straw-colored wine with a pleasing but rather neutral flavor. Parducci in Northern California probably brings out the grape's best features.

Green Hungarian: This is another blending wine from California that is also seen bottled under its own name. Consider it in the same category as Chablis when matching it with seafood.

Soave: Soave is Italy's best white, pale straw in color and light on the palate. It is named for a town rather than a grape as it is a blend of several wines grown on the southernmost foothills of the Alps.

Muscadet: More than five million gallons of wine are produced from the Muscadet grape each year in the Loire Valley of France. And most goes to consumers with one thought in mind: to serve it with seafood.

Fruity Whites

We next turn to the rich, somewhat sweeter wines that blend beautifully with many of the more elaborate ways to prepare seafood. They represent the golden, full wines of the United States, Germany, and Alsace. A trip through either of the two latter areas will give you an idea of the wines' versatility. There they pair up naturally with such spicy foods as sausages, pâté de foie gras, and even sauerkraut.

Here we may consider these young, fresh wines as natural companions to any of the salmon recipes using seasoned stuffings or the dishes with rich, full-flavored sauces. These wines also would stand up nicely to béarnaise or hollandaise sauce. Moving outdoors, a Rhine type or Chenin Blanc would do wonders with barbecued salmon.

Rhine: A bit of a misnomer, this Rhine wine has little to do with Germany's great Rhine River. Generally it is a slightly sweet, blended wine from California. Its best features are that it is inexpensive and is an easy wine to enjoy for those who find Chablis too sharp. Most major wineries make a Rhine-type wine. One fine example is Paul Masson's Rhine Castle.

Riesling: Riesling is a mammoth category, but worth investigating for it will reward you with the best wines of the fruity whites. Let us consider its best possibilities first: wines made from the Johannisberg Riesling grape. The premier white wine grape in the world, it is responsible for the fabled wines of the Rhine and Moselle River areas, Alsace, Switzerland, and California. In the United States, it is most often labeled Johannisberg Riesling and sometimes White Riesling. Domestic varieties contain a pronounced fragrance of flowers and a full, rich flavor. There is a touch of sweetness but it should not be cloying. One of the best examples comes from Washington State under the label Ste. Michelle. In California, the Napa Valley seems to produce the best. Perhaps the world's most honored Rieslings are those from the Rhine or Moselle River vineyards of Germany. Liebfraumilch wins the popularity honors although it is really a blend of many wines. Still, it deserves special mention because it is widely available and relatively inexpensive. Any store will have a good selection of this refreshing, uncomplicated wine. They cost more, of course, but the Rieslings of Germany labeled for individual vineyards will introduce to you the very best. There are many famous names, such as Schloss Johannisberger or Zeller Schwarz Katz, but you will soon discover favorites of your own. Alsace, that storybook land on the German border of France, also does well by the Riesling grape but really shines in the next category of Traminer.

Traminer and Gewürztraminer: Here is where Alsatian wines come into their own. No one could dispute that the Alsatians are among the world's great whites. The wines are very aromatic with a spicy flavor that is irresistible. The word "Gewürz" simply defines the wine as "spicy" Traminer. California also produces some fine Traminers. Almadén, as an example, wins prizes year after year for its distinctive version.

Chenin Blanc: This is one of California's most successful wines. However, its range between sweet and semisweet (it is almost never completely dry) is broad. Mirassou's, for example, is quite sweet while Paul Masson's and Louis Martini's are drier. In the hands of a good vintner, it is a very pleasing wine, full but never syrupy. California, of course, is not alone in its use of Chenin Blanc. France exports great quantities of the famous Vouvray made from the very same grape. The French style tends to be sweet, however, often too sweet for pairing up with our native salmon.

Semillon: While this name on labels is beginning to disappear, the grape is one of the greats in the world of whites. It is used with the Sauvignon Blanc in the Sauternes and Graves wines of France and appears in many California blended wines. It, too, ranges from dry to sweet, but most often is a full-bodied golden wine that lends itself to a wide variety of seafood dishes.

Emerald Riesling: Although this is a Riesling, it is listed separately as the grape is a hybrid developed in California for hotter climates. Only a few wineries produce it, however, Paul Masson does a masterful job under the name Emerald Dry, a lovely fresh wine that should be consumed while young.

Full, Dry Whites

Here are the aristocrats of wine: the deep, full-bodied whites that lend their elegance to the finest of meals. Expensive? Yes, but worth every penny for those special dinners when your favorite guests come. They belong with candlelight, the best china, and carefully prepared food.

Generally speaking, the full, dry whites consist of wines like the Chardonnay and Sauvignon Blanc of California and the great Chablis or White Burgundy of France. They tend to be sharp, pungent wines, often austere in character. This noble trait makes them ideal companions to salmon, pairing up with everything from the simple broiled salmon to the fillet richly doused in sauce.

The great dry whites of the United States and France, despite their reputation, sometimes seem a little harsh to the wine novice. But it is a taste that does not take long to acquire. For many noted connoisseurs, the combination of salmon with a Chardonnay is the absolute ultimate.

Chardonnay: The best Chardonnay has that aged-in-oak taste. It is a golden, full-bodied and fragrant wine that seems to be best from the cooler northern regions such as the Napa Valley. A good introduction will come from any of the noted wineries of California, in particular Robert Mondavi, Beaulieu, Charles Krug, and Beringer. Do not be confused by the label Pinot Chardonnay. It is the same wine.

The Chardonnay grape is international and, although seldom listed on the label, is the one responsible for the classic white wines of France. Chablis, the traditional accompaniment to seafood throughout the world, comes from Chardonnay. A chalky soil in that region of France implants a flinty dryness to the wine that makes it perfect with nearly any seafood. Another famous wine, Pouilly-Fuisse, also is the result of Chardonnay. Despite its sharing the same parent grape with others, Pouilly-Fuisse has its own individual personality in bouquet, taste and texture. Probably the most popular of all French wines in this country, it is relatively easy to find. Finally, the great white Burgundies of the Côte de Beaune are from the Chardonnay. Many consider these wines from the Southern Burgundy area to be the finest dry white wines produced anywhere. The best are from the communes of Chassagne-Montrachet, Puligny-Montrachet, Meursault, Beaune, and Aloxe-Corton. These wines are hard to find and expensive.

Sauvignon Blanc: A tricky one, for it can range from sweet to quite dry. Caution is advised on reading labels, for the drier the better. At its best, the wine is full-bodied, fragrant in the bouquet, and pleasant in the aftertaste. It can also be named Fumé Blanc and Blanc Fumé. We favor the bottlings of Almadén or Robert Mondavi. Christian Brothers makes a superb one called Napa Fumé.

The Sauvignon Blanc pops up in France, particularly in the excellent whites of the Graves region in the Bordeaux area. They are rich, full wines, and quite assertive. Unfortunately, they are often overlooked in favor of the more famous reds of that region. Another white from that grape is Pouilly-Fumé, once reputed to be Marie Antoinette's favorite. It comes from the Loire Valley.

Pinot-Blanc: A relatively obscure grape in California, it has many of the characteristics of Chardonnay but is slightly softer. It is a good substitute for the drier, more severe whites.

Rosé

It would take this entire book to recount the many rosés available on the market today. The best advice we can offer is to reach for the drier ones when selecting a bottle to accompany your salmon. Some rosés are much too sweet for the subtle flavor of fish. In California, the best rosés are made from higher quality grapes and then labeled under the varietal names. Zinfandel Rosé, for example, usually assures the consumer of something better than the usual vin rosé. Likewise, there are drier rosés made from Cabernet Sauvignon, Gamay, Petite Sirah, and the popular Grenache. Mondavi produces a fine Gamay Rosé and Pedroncelli has a winner with its Zinfandel Rosé.

Imported rosés are popular on the market as well. Perhaps the most preferred are the rosés of Portugal, which are ideal with seasoned foods. Mateus, in the distinctive rounded bottle, is a best seller, although there are other fine ones to be found. France produces at least two very fine rosés that would be appropriate with salmon. They are the Tavel, a light crimson wine with plenty of taste, and the paler but refreshing Anjou. In fact, the color of Anjou is often described as being salmon, a happy and tasty coincidence.

Tom Stockley is the author of *101 Wines (under $5)* and a columnist for *The Seattle Times.*

Index

Other Books from Pacific Search Press

Asparagus: The Sparrowgrass Cookbook by Autumn Stanley
Bone Appétit! Natural Food for Pets by Frances Sheridan Goulart
Butterflies Afield in the Pacific Northwest
    by William Neill/Douglas Hepburn, photography
The Carrot Cookbook by Ann Saling
Cascade Companion
    by Susan Schwartz/Bob and Ira Spring, photography
Common Seaweeds of the Pacific Coast by J. Robert Waaland
The Crawfish Cookbook by Norma S. Upson
Cross-Country Downhill and Other Nordic Mountain
    Skiing Techniques by Steve Barnett
The Dogfish Cookbook by Russ Mohney
Fire and Ice: The Cascade Volcanoes by Stephen L. Harris
The Green Tomato Cookbook by Paula Simmons
Little Mammals of the Pacific Northwest by Ellen B. Kritzman
Living Shores of the Pacific Northwest
    by Lynwood Smith/Bernard Nist, photography
Make It and Take It: Homemade Gear for Camp and Trail
    by Russ Mohney
Messages from the Shore by Victor B. Scheffer
Minnie Rose Lovgreen's Recipe for Raising Chickens
    by Minnie Rose Lovgreen
Rhubarb Renaissance: A Cookbook by Ann Saling
Sleek & Savage: North America's Weasel Family
    by Delphine Haley
Spinning and Weaving with Wool by Paula Simmons
Why Wild Edibles? The Joys of Finding, Fixing, and Tasting
    by Russ Mohney
Wild Mushroom Recipes by Puget Sound Mycological Society
Wild Shrubs: Finding and Growing Your Own by Joy Spurr
The Zucchini Cookbook by Paula Simmons